WAGES, LABOUR AND REGIONAL DEVELOPMENT IN BRAZIL

Wages, Labour and Regional Development in Brazil

WILLIAM D. SAVEDOFF
Inter-American Development Bank

Avebury

Aldershot • Brookfield USA • Hong Kong • Singapore • Sydney

Published by
Avebury
Ashgate Publishing Limited
Gower House
Croft Road
Aldershot
Hants GU11 3HR
England

Ashgate Publishing Company
Old Post Road
Brookfield
Vermont 05036
USA

British Library Cataloguing in Publication Data

Savedoff, William D.
    Wages, Labour and Regional Development
    in Brazil
    I. Title
    338.16096891

ISBN 1 85628 964 8

Library of Congress Catalog Card Number: 95-79655

HD
5004
.528
1995

Printed and bound by Athenæum Press Ltd.,
Gateshead, Tyne & Wear.

Contents

Figures and tables

Acknowledgements

I would like to thank the Institute for the Study of World Politics (Washington, DC) for the funding that made this research possible, and the Instituto de Pesquisas Econômicas e Sociais (IPEA/INPES) of the Secretary of Planning in Rio de Janeiro which provided facilities and access to data. This research benefitted from the comments, criticism and suggestions of numerous friends and colleagues, especially Ricardo Pães de Barros, David Lam, Guilherme Sedlacek, Lauro Ramos and my advisors Peter Doeringer and Kevin Lang. Werner Baer and Douglas Wissoker made helpful comments on different drafts. I am also grateful to the many people who accepted my requests for interviews in both Rio de Janeiro and Recife, to whom I remain greatly indebted.

1 Introduction: A framework for analyzing regional wage differentials

Income varies widely across Brazil's diverse regions, as in many other countries. The degree of regional inequality, however, is more acute than elsewhere.[1] In the Northeast, where a majority of Brazil's impoverished citizens reside, wages are significantly lower than in the South and Southeast. An unskilled worker in the Northeast can almost double his or her earnings by obtaining comparable work in São Paulo. The persistence of large wage differentials challenges standard market theories of the labour market that would predict a regional convergence of wages in Brazil and necessitates further investigation in terms of dynamic patterns of regional differentiation.

This book investigates whether the work force in Brazil is geographically segmented by analyzing variation in workers' earnings. It finds that standard market explanations for regional wage disparities, such as variations in the cost of living or the quality of the workforce, can explain only a part of the disparities. The regional composition and specificities of labour demand also contribute significantly to the pattern of regional wage differences. The study concludes that geographical obstacles to factor flows are not significant in Brazil. Rather, the disparities in wages reflect a dynamic of labour flows, demographics, and employment growth which persistently sustain wage differences across regions in spite of increasing national economic integration.

1

Approaches to regional differentials

Regional wage differentials have been variously ascribed to differences in productivity, compensating differentials, and rents. In a dynamic framework, these differentials will converge or diverge depending on the processes which have sustained them in the past. Approaches which emphasize market processes argue that wage differences are self-limiting, that they create incentives and encourage decisions which will, given time, ultimately diminish the gap. Other approaches — for example, those emphasizing political and social determinants of regional growth, unequal exchange, or increasing returns in production — tend to argue that wage differences may persist and even grow.

The first major reason that wages may differ across regions is that people may be paid higher when their work is more productive. These differences in productivity themselves can have three distinct sources — worker skills, job characteristics, and regionally captured externalities.

A variety of studies focus on differences in workers. If workers are systematically more productive in one region than another, they may be better remunerated. This would be the case when a particular region enjoys a more highly educated or healthier workforce. Similarly, if output from jobs in one region are more productive because of larger capital investment or better quality inputs, then once again wage differences would be expected. This may be clearest in the simple case of equally skilled farmers tilling soils with different fertility. It would also apply to urban economies with different levels of capital investment and technologies. Finally, regional productivity differences may result not from any individual attribute of individuals, or any isolated characteristic of jobs, but rather from combined regional effects resulting from scale or composition. For example, economies of agglomeration may reduce input costs and raise productivity across many firms. When the costs of expensive public infrastructure (energy, water, transportation) are more widely shared, average costs can be reduced and productivity increased. In each case, higher productivity from worker skills, job characteristics, or regional externalities can increase wages relative to other regions.

In a static framework, the identification of productivity differences would be sufficient to explain differences in earnings across regions. But from a more realistic, dynamic perspective, the productivity and earnings differences might or might not be sustainable. Countervailing processes can erode regional wage differentials if the spatial distribution of workers changes with migration, technology, or investment. For example, if productivity differences are caused by differences in capital investment, then workers in lower paid regions would have an incentive to migrate, thereby

2

driving wages down in the higher wage region. Other regional differences, however, might encourage the persistence of wage differentials even in the presence of migration flows. For example, the existence of scale economies, whereby firms face declining average costs of production as output and scale increase, could sustain a process of increasing productivity and maintain regional wage differentials so long as the effects of increasing returns to employing the expanding labour force remain sufficiently large.

The second broad reason for regional wage differences is that of compensating differentials, which arises from the fact that nominal wages are imperfect accounting units. Even if there were no productivity differentials, nominal wages could still emerge as a reflection of the different *value* of nominal currency to workers in different regions. Nominal wage disparities in this view might simply reflect differences in the cost of living, i.e., regional price levels. Regional amenities may also affect workers' choice of residence. Regions differ in climate, topography, and land use. They also differ in terms of the provision of public goods. As long as workers systematically prefer certain amenities which are unevenly distributed spatially, nominal wage differences may reflect compensation for those in relatively less favored areas.

In a static framework, such regional amenity or cost of living differences can explain wage gaps. In a dynamic framework, however, the explanation is not satisfactory because (i) the amenity differences are themselves an outcome of some region-specific process (e.g., the creation of public goods), and (ii) if the cost of maintaining workers is lower in one region, the expansion or relocation of firms in the lower cost region would tend to equalize nominal differences.

Third and final, if wage earning differences exist after accounting for productivity and 'accounting' differences, wages may differ across regions because of rents. For example, rents can arise from temporarily unforeseen fluctuations in supply and demand (broadly considered, .e.g., shifts in bargaining strength could be evaluated as a shift in the reservation wage, and hence in the labour supply curve). These rents can be maintained over time, though, only in the presence of some kind of barriers. The most common explanation for persistent regional wage differentials is transaction costs: transportation and relocation costs which discourage workers from taking full advantage of high wage regions; relocation costs which discourage firms from moving to lower wage regions; lack of information which keeps agents from being aware of better opportunities in other regions; or uncertainty which discourages risk-averse agents from acting upon apparent incentives to move (e.g., expectations of unemployment).

Regional rents can also be maintained by intraregional segmentation of the labour market. If agents are extremely well-informed about employment opportunities and wages in different regions and if certain jobs are rationed then rents can be maintained even in the presence of strong market integration. Jobs can be rationed as a result of any process which keeps wages above the market-clearing level, such as efficiency wages, union contracts, government wage policy, or firm-specific job training.

It is important to note that nominal wage differences in themselves are not evidence against the existence of a single price in the labour market from the workers' perspective. As noted above, an individual would not be motivated to migrate to a higher nominal wage area if the cost of living in that area were comparably higher. On the other hand, the persistence of nominal wage differentials does raise questions about the *demand* side of the labour market. Why would firms producing tradeable goods continue to produce in high nominal wage areas when labour costs could be reduced by relocating or expanding elsewhere?

The responses for this demand side question may also vary, but all involve theories of the firm or production. If it were observed that firms do not seek to expand in low wage areas, this could be attributed to characteristics of business owners and their personal motivations for locating in a particular region, or from other regional aspects which affect their costs. In either case, continuing nominal differentials raise questions about the optimal allocation of both production and labour.

The possibility of *real* and *nominal* wage differentials raises distinct issues. Under conditions of perfectly competitive and perfectly integrated markets, arbitrage on the demand and supply sides of the labour market would erase both nominal and real wage differences. In the absence of perfect arbitrage, however, it is entirely possible for these two 'values' to diverge. Under conditions in which firms are immobile but individual workers are perfectly mobile and seeking the highest wage, nominal wages might differ across regions while real wages remain equal. Conversely, if firms are mobile and seek out regions with low nominal wage costs and individual workers are obstructed from following the incentives of higher real wages, real wage differences might occur alongside perfectly equal nominal wages. With imperfect arbitrage on the demand and supply sides of the labour market, it is entirely possible, for example, for a region to be simultaneously a high nominal wage and low real wage area. Consequently, estimation and discussion of regional wage differentials must distinguish the analysis of real and nominal wage differentials because they represent evidence of distinct processes of arbitrage in the labour market.

Relevant studies on Brazil and other countries

Numerous studies have addressed regional wage differences in Brazil and other countries, but none have addressed all of the issues raised above in analyzing regional wage gaps in Brazil.

Productivity differences are frequently cited as an explanation for the regional gap in wages. Lacking direct measures of individual productivity, years of schooling is generally used as a proxy for worker quality (Dabos and Psacharopoulos 1987, Behrman and Birdsall 1983). In such studies, regional differences in wages remain robust after controlling for observed individual characteristics. Less information is available relating wages and job-related productivity, although sectoral productivity itself has been analyzed in depth (Hoffman 1990, Considera 1986, Ablas and Fava 1985). Regional productivity differences resulting from scale economies or externalities are theoretically promising as explanations for regional wage differences because they emphasize attributes which are regionally specific — the size of local markets and locally-captured externalities.[2] The literature which addresses this issue in Brazil, however, has generally focused on unequal exchange (Ablas and Fava 1985) with fairly weak empirical data.

Other approaches, also focusing on productivity differences, see regional wage variation as a result of underlying regional differences which are continually reproduced in spite of the increasing national integration of markets — and sometimes because of this increasing integration. Such processes can be presented within neoclassical growth models which show the persistence of regional wage disparities as long as elasticities of substitution or rates of technical change differ across regions (Batra and Scully 1972). It can also result from historically contingent processes (Baer 1964, Furtado 1976). For example, Werner Baer argues that the Southeast was favored by net flows of private capital, the internal balance of trade, and exchange rate policies that subsidized the import-substituting industries of the Southeast. Furthermore, the net impact of migration had been negative for the Northeast, draining the region of its skilled and educated workers (Baer 1964).[3] A dynamic view of the recreation of regional wage disparities is also frequently presented in frameworks emphasizing class relations and the political economy of Brazilian development (Storper 1984, Mitchell 1981). Such is the case in Storper's argument that geographical dispersion of capital is a class strategy to reduce average wages. He argues that in Brazil, capital remained concentrated in the Southeast because government repression of labour impeded worker mobilization which would otherwise have forced businesses to decentralize their activities.

Other authors have emphasized the different value of nominal wages across regions. As noted above, nominal wage differences may reflect differences in the cost of living, i.e., regional price levels. This approach is taken by Vinod Thomas (1987:267) in his appraisal of regional wage differentials, arguing that they predominantly, if not solely, reflect the difference in cost of living across regions. By implication, nominal wage differences will converge only to the degree that price levels and spatial distribution of productivity equalize.

The most common explanation for regional wage differences views them essentially as temporary rents. Such approaches argue that regional wage differentials occur because regional labour markets are relatively isolated from one another, and have varying conditions of supply and demand (Morley 1984, Pfefferman and Webb 1982, Schmitz 1985:74). Such a view predicts that regional wage differentials will diminish over time to the degree that increasing integration of the national economy and expansion of factor flows bring about a convergence in supply and demand conditions across the different regions. Williamson went even further by classifying conditions which bring about an equalization of regional income gaps as economic growth evolves, and predicted that Brazil had passed its greatest level of spatial inequality (Williamson 1965).

Many of these views are explicitly considered in studies that focus specifically on regional wage differences in Latin America. In an analysis of Colombian census data, Fields and Schultz found that,

> . . . half the interregional differences . . . can be explained simply in terms of education and age. Still, much remains to be accounted for by, on the one hand, other aspects of workers' skills, job experience, and training, and, on the other hand, by long-run factor market distortions and short run quasi-rents to workers in specific regional labour markets. Fields and Schultz, p. 459.

Heckman and Hotz (1986) studied a sample of Panamanian males and found large regional differences in earnings across twelve regions. They suggested that returns do not equalize across regions because of (1) different labour demand conditions, and (2) different labour supply conditions with mobility costs. In a study of Guatemalan household survey data, This author also found significant regional differences in income which could not be attributed to personal characteristics or regional differences in sectoral composition of employment.[4]

Regional wage differences, then, have been approached in a variety of ways. Underlying all these approaches are debates over whether the nominal wage variation reflects real variation in productivity, compensating differentials, or rents received by workers in privileged areas — either permanently as in dynamic theories of reproduced disparities or temporarily as in theories of market disequilibrium.

Framework

This study will use a market model as a framework for organizing the information related to regional wage differentials. This does not mean that the study starts by assuming that market forces operate to determine wages in Brazil. Rather, the concept of a market is used as a null model against which evidence can be tested and considered. As will be seen, there is evidence of outcomes which are not fully consistent with the operation of perfect markets. Nevertheless, the model is still an excellent tool for organizing information and emphasizing certain social processes that may reflect individual optimizing behaviour.

The framework utilized here will address systematically the alternative explanations discussed above. The observation of different nominal wages across subgroups of the labour force can be compared with evidence of differences in productivity and compensating differentials. Any real wage difference that cannot be attributed to these two broad factors must be evidence of rents.

In the specific case of regional wage differentials, productivity may differ systematically across regions due to variation in the quality of the labour force or characteristics of employment.[5] Compensating differentials include an enormous range of factors, anything which changes the utility-value of a given nominal wage — be it the cost of living, working conditions, access to public services, environment, culture, or family ties, etc. Finally, if there are real and/or nominal regional wage differences that cannot be attributed to productivity differentials, then the market framework leads to the following questions: Why don't people move from low wage to high wage regions in sufficient numbers to shift relative labour supplies and bring about real wage equalization? Why don't firms move from high wage to low wage regions in sufficient numbers to shift relative labour demand conditions and equalize nominal wages? Why doesn't trade specialization occur, raising labour demand in low wage regions by specializing in labour-intensive production? Microeconomic theory has shown that there are numerous mechanisms of private incentive that would operate to equalize prices in a given market, even in the presence of obstacles or constraints to mobility in any particular sector.[6] The persistence of regional wage differences in spite of relatively unconstrained behaviour recommends a qualification of static market perspectives on the labour market and yields insights into the determination of wages through the resulting regionally comparative findings.

7

This study uses household survey data to estimate regional wage differentials across Brazil's nine major metropolitan regions by controlling for personal characteristics correlated with labour quality and for employment characteristics correlated with sector and occupation. It differs from previous studies in several important ways. First, it does not restrict the analysis to productivity differences measured by personal characteristics alone (e.g., age, education) but specifically addresses regional composition of labour demand. Second, the question of price differences and compensating differentials are explicitly addressed. Third, previous studies have generally used a single cross-section sample and could not therefore rule out the possibility of temporary disequilibria as an explanation for the observed regional wage differentials. This study, by contrast, uses Brazilian household surveys from 1976 to 1987 to show that the results are not a one time aberration for a particular year. It includes additional data on regional wage differences from 1950 to 1980 which show considerable stability over this longer period. Finally, the study goes further in incorporating evidence from interviews regarding wage-setting strategies by firms and agents' perceptions of regional advantages.

The following chapter presents an overview of Brazil's economic development and its nine major metropolitan regions. Chapter 3 provides an overview of historical trends which may influence regional wage levels and contribute to geographic disparities. The subsequent three chapters estimate regional wage differentials and analyze them from a static perspective: Chapter 4 explains the methodology for an econometric estimation of regional nominal wage differentials using a sample from 1985; Chapter 5 presents the findings of this econometric analysis for men in the urban labour force, and Chapter 6 estimates regional wage differentials for subsamples and alternative samples in order to evaluate the strength of the initial findings. Chapter 7 then discusses the problems raised by the apparent arbitrage opportunities, specifically addressing variation in price levels and the possibility of compensating differentials for workers, and agglomeration economies and nonlabour costs for firms.

Chapters 8 and 9 address the regional wage differences in a dynamic context. Chapter 8 focuses on a recent 10-year period (1976 to 1987), estimating the regional wage differentials with household survey data and confronting them with data on local labour market conditions. Chapter 9 takes a longer term perspective (1950-1980) to show the persistence of these wage differences and consider the implications in light of evidence on spatial patterns of economic development. The concluding chapter returns to the framework presented here and evaluates the various explanations, as well as considers their implications for wage determination and public policy in Brazil.

Notes

1. Consider the United States, Italy, and India in works by Sahling and Smith (1983), Dunford (1986), and Mathur (1982). Williamson (1965) compares Brazil and twenty-three other countries.

2. Consider, for example, the model of increasing returns in production presented in Murphy et al (1989).

3. This seems to be continuing in the 1970s and 1980s. See Chapter 3 and Schmertmann (1988).

4. In Guatemala, I used arbitrary state boundaries as regional categories and found the wage differences to be comparable across all labour classes (employed, self-employed, white collar, blue collar). I argued that in this case, Guatemala's history of political repression against labour along with extreme concentration of control over labor in rural areas create restrictions to labor mobility and account for the regional variation in earnings (Savedoff 1987).

5. Setting aside the question of interaction between the two, such as specific job training.

6. The classic theorem in this case is presented in W.F. Stolper and P.A. Samuelson 1948, "Protection and Real Wages", *Review of Economic Statistics*, November 1941 and P.A. Samuelson, "International Trade and the Equalisation of Factor Prices", *Economic Journal*, June.

2 Brazilian economic development and the nine major metropolitan regions

Brazil is the world's fifth largest country in size, and the tenth largest economy as measured by GNP. Its incredibly fast pace of economic growth over this century allowed it to surpass Argentina as the continent's major economy. More importantly, the last 40 years have transformed Brazil's economy. In 1950, Brazil still relied on a single primary export crop — coffee — for the majority of its foreign earnings; today, manufactures and processed goods represent more than two-thirds of Brazilian exports and include such products of advanced technology as training airplanes for the British Royal Air Force. In only thirty years, between 1950 and 1980, Brazil urbanized, industrialized, diversified, and developed a nationally articulated economy.

This chapter summarizes Brazil's historical economic development. It also presents brief descriptions of the nine major metropolitan regions which will be analyzed in this book. Later chapters will expand upon the processes and contrasts discussed below.

A brief socioeconomic history of Brazil

Brazil was settled by the Portuguese in the 1600s, serving as a source of dyes and exotic woods, and later as a source of sugar. The indigenous populations were sparse and driven out of coastal areas by European settlement. The small population grew fairly steadily with immigration from Europe and the forced transportation of Africans to work as slaves in the expanding colonial economy.

10

In 1821, Brazil became an independent empire, ruled by the Portuguese heir to the throne until he was forced to abdicate in favor of his native-born son. During the 19th century, the sugar-producing sectors went into a pronounced decline, slavery was questioned and eventually abolished (1888), the monarchy was overthrown (1889), and coffee became the country's dominant economic activity. European immigration grew rapidly in the late 19th century due to public subsidies and a coffee boom which helped drive a dramatic pace of economic growth through the 1920s. During this period, São Paulo gained importance over previous population and economic centres. Significant amounts of earnings from coffee exports were channeled into investment in Brazil's nascent industries, setting the foundations for later industrial expansion.

The coffee boom ended in 1930 when international coffee prices plummeted. This crisis coincided with a conflict among regional ruling groups over federal power. Out of this conflict, Getulio Vargas became president. With military backing, Vargas was proclaimed president in 1930. A military coup in 1937 kept him in power until 1945. During this period (1930-1945), industrial production grew rapidly, a modern urban labour force was formed in the major cities, and the state expanded to provide public infrastructure as well as producing key industrial inputs such as oil and steel. The government also expanded its regulation and repression of workers who had been actively mobilizing in the early part of the century. The Vargas government (1930-1945) explicitly sought to control growing labour mobilization through a strategy of cooptation, basing much of its legislation on Mussolini's fascist labour codes. For example, the labour laws enacted during this period sought to forestall worker organization by geographically fragmenting unions and by setting strict requirements for recognition by the Ministry of Labour.

Since World War II, Brazil has gone through three distinct political stages and has now entered a fourth. The first, from 1947 to 1964 was a period of elected governments. The second phase began in 1964 with a military coup and a period of repressive military rule. From the late 1970s until 1990, the military governments presided over a transition toward civilian rule which culminated in 1990 with a national direct election for president.

The entire post-war period was one of remarkable socioeconomic change. Population growth continued at about 2.6% per year, almost tripling the population from approximately 40 million in 1940 to over 110 million by 1980. The country became predominantly urban in this same period. Between 1950 and 1980, the urban share of the population increased from 36% to 67%. Although the growth of urban population in the 1950s was strongly affected by rural-urban migration, the pace of urban growth since

1970 has been largely driven by natural increase in the cities themselves, in spite of rapid declines in fertility over the same period.[1]

Rapid industrialization after 1950 also changed the structure of Brazil's economic activities and exports. Until 1950, coffee accounted for a majority of the country's foreign exchange earnings. By 1980, however, some two-thirds of export earnings came from manufactured and processed goods. The creation of national steel, automobile, aviation, and consumer electronics industries were dramatic examples of industrial expansion, but were also accompanied by growth in more traditional industries such as textiles, footwear, and clothing. Agricultural expansion was slower but nonetheless substantial, with the appearance of entirely new products such as orange concentrate and soybeans. Economic growth during this period averaged 7% per year, yielding per capita increases in national income of approximately 4%.

The period from 1967 to 1973 has been called a period of 'miracle economic growth'. GNP expanded 11% annually during this time.[2] The 1973 oil shock created problems for the external accounts because of the country's heavy dependence upon petroleum imports. Growth was maintained until 1982 through a combination of external borrowing and government spending. The debt crisis in 1982 ended this growth phase and culminated in a severe recession. In 1985, growth resumed with an acceleration of inflation. Since 1986, the country has been subjected to a variety of orthodox and heterodox stabilization plans to address the country's high and accelerating rates of inflation.

Labour unions became increasingly active and politically powerful during the brief period of democratic elections of the 1950s. Union activities virtually ceased, however, after the strikes of 1968 due to heavy repression by the military regime. Only in 1978 did the labour movement reemerge to confront the military, winning important concessions and recognition from firms. Since 1978, the labour movement has grown and expanded. Its strength, however, is largely concentrated in the Southeast, especially in São Paulo. The 1978 strikes began in São Paulo's industrial centres, where the major automobile producers are concentrated, and spread from there to Rio and Belo Horizonte. The strongest unions in the private sector continue to be the metallurgical and electrical unions of São Paulo. The union movements have become nationally organized, establishing two national labour federations in the early 1980s: CUT and the CGT.[3] Also, the Workers Party (Partido dos Trabalhadores) was founded in 1981 by leaders of the 1978 strikes. Luís Inácio Lula da Silva, one of these leaders, ran for president in Brazil's first direct presidential elections since the 1964 coup and came in second place with 47.5% of the votes cast. He also polled second in the elections of November 1995.

Brazil continues to have strong regional differences. The largest contrasts are between the rural and urban areas where access to public infrastructure and income gaps are particularly high. However, the greatest differences are not easily captured in numbers. Low-income people in rural areas are subject to violence. Land disputes have killed hundreds of people in the last 10 years. The urban poor are also victims of violence, but the kinds and sources of violence differ considerably. Problems relating to access to education, water, and housing, are common to both urban poor and rural poor, but the barriers to be overcome differ. In addition, there are substantial differences between the major urban areas which will be discussed below.

The nine major metropolitan regions

This section briefly describes Brazil's nine major metropolitan regions,[4] establishing the boundaries of the sample studied in this book for reasons which will be discussed in Chapter 4. Before looking at the cities individually, however, it is worth considering that the regional differences in wages highlight a strong contrast in their labour market outcomes. Median hourly wages for each major city are presented in Table 2.1, showing the substantial regional differences.[5] The median in Fortaleza is half the value of the median in São Paulo. Recife is also extremely low in this comparison with a median wage of $0.41/hour.[6] Belém and Belo Horizonte are also below the national median with wages at approximately $0.51/hour. Rio de Janeiro and Salvador have medians which match the national median, while Curitiba and Porto Alegre are somewhat above ($0.60/hour and $0.64/hour, respectively).

Table 2.1 also shows the coefficient of variation as a summary measure for intra-regional wage dispersion. It is apparent that wage inequality is inversely proportional to the wage level — that is, the cities with lower wages have a more unequal distribution of wages. São Paulo with the highest median wage has the lowest coefficient of variation (1.39), whereas Fortaleza, Recife, Belém, and Belo Horizonte all have higher variation. This relationship between low wages and high income inequality has also been verified in other studies (Almeida 1989).

13

Table 2.1
Comparison of hourly wages by metropolitan region
Male employees and self-employed — 1985

Metropolitan Region	Median Hourly Wage (US$/hour)	Coefficient of Variation
Belém	0.51	1.69
Fortaleza	0.37	1.73
Recife	0.41	1.71
Salvador	0.53	1.58
Belo Horizonte	0.51	1.66
Rio de Janeiro	0.53	1.56
São Paulo	0.71	1.39
Curitiba	0.60	1.59
Porto Alegre	0.64	1.63
All	0.53	1.52

Note: Conversion is at official exchange rate October 1, 1985 of Cr$7,830/US$ as reported in *Conjuntura Econômica*, Jan. 1986. Coefficient of Variation is the ratio of the standard deviation to the mean.
Source: Author's tabulations from the IBGE's PNAD data, 1985.

Although the remainder of the text emphasizes regional wage *differences* measured in relative terms, it is important to recognize that the wage *levels* being discussed are extremely low. The median wage in São Paulo was twice that of Fortaleza, but this median wage was still only 71 cents per hour in 1985 — a year of relative prosperity. More than half of the working Brazilian males surveyed earned less than this wage.

The low absolute level of pay has various contradictory implications for the puzzle of regional wage differences. On the one hand, a 20% difference at subsistence levels should be a stronger encouragement to migration than a 20% difference at more sustainable levels of living standard since the low absolute wage represents an impulse to leave in addition to the attraction of the higher wage elsewhere. On the other hand, at low absolute levels of pay it is difficult for workers to accumulate enough resources to migrate or to risk unemployment in a new city. Finally, the low absolute level of pay may help explain why businesses in the country's wealthy southeast do not seem to move to low wage areas. If labour costs are already a small share of production costs — and there is evidence of declining labour shares since the 1950s (Considera 1986) — then lack of capital flows to low-wage areas would not contradict the premise that firms operate rationally to maximize profits.

Figure 2.1 shows the location of the nine cities covered in this study. They account for almost one-third of Brazil's population and more than 60% of its measured economic output. Some general characteristics of the cities are presented in Tables 2.2 and 2.3. The cities will be discussed from North to South, beginning with Belém. For ease in presentation, this order will be maintained in all of the tables.

Table 2.2
Selected characteristics of Brazil's metropolitan regions, 1985

Metropolitan Region	Resident Population	LFPR	Productivity (1980)	Mean Education (Years)
Belém	1,077,858	50.2%	986	5.59
Fortaleza	1,868,835	54.6%	904	4.76
Recife	2,695,238	49.5%	1,524	4.79
Salvador	2,110,770	54.2%	3,037	5.37
Belo Horizonte	3,085,594	55.3%	2,216	5.31
Rio de Janeiro	10,244,799	54.0%	2,151	5.68
São Paulo	15,335,857	58.0%	2,252	5.41
Curitiba	1,791,770	56.8%	2,199	5.43
Porto Alegre	2,616,051	58.0%	1,571	5.79

Notes:
LFPR = Labour Force Participation Rate as share of population 10 years and older.
Productivity = Output per production worker in manufacturing in Cr$1,000/worker, for corresponding states, not metropolitan regions.
Mean Education = Estimated mean years of schooling for the population 10 years and older.
Source: Calculated from IBGE, PNAD 1985; and IBGE *Censo Industrial* 1980.

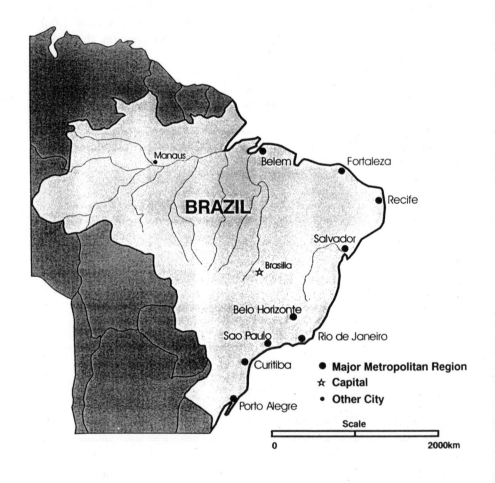

Figure 2.1 Brazil's nine major metropolitan regions

16

Table 2.3

Composition of occupied labour force (%)

| Metropolitan Region | Share of economically active population 10 years and older | | |
	Manufacturing	Public Administration	Less Than Minimum Wage
Belém	10.3	8.3	23.1
Fortaleza	17.1	6.7	32.2
Recife	13.4	6.2	30.7
Salvador	9.9	7.9	26.7
Belo Horizonte	16.4	5.2	27.9
Rio de Janeiro	16.1	7.2	24.1
São Paulo	31.7	3.6	11.4
Curitiba	20.0	5.8	17.6
Porto Alegre	25.6	6.2	14.7

Source: Calculated from PNAD 1985.

Belém is the northernmost metropolitan region, located at the mouth of the Amazon River in the state of Pará. It expanded most rapidly at the turn of the century as a consequence of a boom in rubber exports. Belém is relatively isolated compared to the other metropolitan regions; historically, it was more closely linked to Europe and the United States through trade than it was to the other cities of Brazil. Since the 1950s, it has become steadily more integrated with the rest of the economy, but physical distance alone makes transportation costly. Federal subsidies and price controls therefore strongly affect the price level in Belém, as a large share of its goods are imported from other parts of Brazil. In some years, the price level jumps precipitously because of scarcities in basic food items such as beans.[7]

Belém is the smallest of the metropolitan regions, with a resident population of 1,077,858 and a labour force of 408,338 in 1985. It also had the second lowest labour force participation rate — 50.2% for the population over 10 years old. Industrial employment represented a mere 10% of all economically active people, and output per worker in industry was second lowest, after Fortaleza.

Fortaleza is located on the coast of the state of Ceará in Brazil's Northeast. It had a resident population of 1,868,835 and a work force of 751,430 in 1985. Industrial employment accounts for some 17% of the economically active population, higher than the share in Rio de Janeiro. Nevertheless, Fortaleza displays the lowest productivity in manufacturing of all the metropolitan regions, roughly 40% of the productivity in São Paulo and only 60% of the productivity in the nearby state of Pernambuco. Fortaleza periodically receives heavy migration from the *sertão*, or backlands, which are subject to cycles of drought. The *flagelados*, migrants who flee the backlands in times of drought, filled the city in the early 1980s, and the federal government responded with numerous public works programmes to generate employment. The influx dissipated in the mid-1980s, partly through return migration; partly through migration to rural settlements in the Amazon; and partly through migration to other major cities such as Recife, Salvador, Rio de Janeiro, and São Paulo. Fortaleza has the highest degree of informal activities by almost any measure: some 32% of the labour force earn less than one minimum wage[8] and almost half of all employees work without the legal benefits and protection associated with having a work card.

Recife is the capital of Pernambuco, also located in the Northeast. Recife was the centre of struggle between the Dutch, French and Portuguese in the 1600s, and the world's major sugar producer in that period. It was the first key economic centre in the colony, but later lost preeminence to Salvador. In 1985, Recife had a resident population of 2,695,238 with a work force of 1,002,276. Recife attracts a large flow of migrants from smaller cities in the Northeast, has the lowest labour force participation rate (49.5%), and a high share of informal activities (35% of employees have no work card, and 47% of the labour force is not enrolled in social security programmes). Recife has two large industrial parks within the metropolitan area which are strong in textiles, but have more recently entered mechanical and electronic assembly. Some 13% of the work force is employed in manufacturing, a sector which has benefitted from public investment in energy and federal fiscal incentives since the 1970s.

Salvador is the next metropolitan area along the coast, still part of the Northeast, and capital of the state of Bahia. Its deep harbour and enormous bay were an early inducement to Portuguese settlement, and the city soon became the headquarters for the Brazilian colony. Salvador steadily lost influence as the sugar economy declined in the 1700s, to be replaced by Rio

18

de Janeiro and São Paulo which benefitted from the expansion of coffee. Salvador has the highest concentration of Blacks of any city in Brazil due to the heritage of slavery. In 1985, Salvador had a resident population of 2,110,770 and a work force of 849,128. Its share of industrial employment is low (9.9%) but highly productive. In fact, manufacturing in Salvador produced greater output per worker than São Paulo because its industry is less diversified and the sectors which have grown recently employ particularly capital-intensive techniques (Almeida 1981). Salvador has benefitted disproportionately from the federal government's fiscal incentives for investment in the Northeast, as well as direct government projects such as the petrochemical pole of Camaçari[9] and the hydroelectric projects along the São Francisco River begun in the early 1970s. Consequently, Salvador has become a dynamic part of the national economy.

Belo Horizonte is in the country's Southeast, in the mountains of the state of Minas Gerais. It was traditionally a centre for mining and cattle, but more recently has seen an expansion of industry. It is Brazil's third largest city with a resident population of 3,085,594 in 1985, and a labour force of 1,290,769. Industrial employment accounts for 16.4% of the occupied labour force, and productivity in manufacturing is comparable to that of Rio or São Paulo. Minas Gerais has been a steady source of migrants to Rio and São Paulo, but the city of Belo Horizonte has also grown by attracting people from surrounding smaller cities. More recently, Belo Horizonte may have become a dynamic part of an expanding axis of industrial expansion spreading northward from São Paulo (Egler 1986).

Rio de Janeiro is one of Brazil's most intriguing cities because of its enormous advantages but continual decay. Located on the coast of the Southeast in the state of Rio de Janeiro, its ample protected bay and surrounding fertile valleys allowed it to surpass Salvador as the colony's headquarters in the 18th century. The Portuguese kingdom was even seated here during the Napoleonic wars. At the turn of the century, Rio had advantages comparable to São Paulo in terms of capital and labour, and was perhaps even more favored in terms of transportation and infrastructure. It had comparable shares of coffee production and industrial output. Nevertheless, as agriculture stagnated and industrialization proceeded slowly, Rio lost its leading role to São Paulo some time around the turn of the century. Employment related to the federal government increased its importance to the city until 1960 when the federal capital moved out of Rio to Brasília. The share of public employment in Rio's metropolitan region, however, remains high because much of the federal employment and state enterprise headquarters remained while other sectors only grew slowly. In 1975, the metropolitan region which had been a separate state, was fused with the surrounding State of Rio de Janeiro. This integration diffused much of the city's resources and shifted political-economic power within the area.

Rio is Brazil's second largest city with a resident population of 10,244,779 and a labour force of 4,406,467 in 1985. Its industry accounts for only 16.1% of the occupied work force, and produces only 9% of national industrial output even though Rio produced more than one-quarter of industrial output in the 1920s. Rio has a particularly high share of employment in services (24.5%), more than São Paulo (19.3%) and comparable to Recife (24.3%). Almost one-quarter of the labour force earn less than the minimum wage, comparable to Belém and more than double the share in São Paulo. Productivity in manufacturing is very close to the national average.

São Paulo is the largest, most dynamic city in Brazil. It assumed this role in the 1920s and has retained its predominance since then. Its resident population was 15,335,857 in 1985, with a labour force of 6,840,324. Its labour force participation rate of 58% is rivalled only by Porto Alegre. A remarkable 31.7% of the occupied work force is employed in manufacturing, much higher than any other city. Average productivity is lower than in Salvador only because manufacturing in São Paulo is so much more diversified. São Paulo manufactures more than 40% of Brazil's total output in all but four of twenty industrial sectors (Ablas and Fava 1985, Table 1.16). The city by itself accounts for fully one-quarter of the nation's GDP. It has benefitted continually from government export incentives, import licenses, and infrastructural investment. In the 1970s, the large Itaipú hydroelectric project was specifically undertaken to provide power for the São Paulo economy. Although the 1970s showed signs of decentralization in economic activity out of São Paulo, much of this economic activity has moved into the State of São Paulo's smaller cities or northward in an axis toward Belo Horizonte and beyond toward Brasília (Egler 1986).

Curitiba is located in the South. It is another inland city, situated in the highlands of the state of Paraná. Its resident population was 1,791,770 in 1985, with a labour force of 768,255. Its population, like Porto Alegre, is dominated by people of European descent who immigrated to Brazil after the end of slavery in 1888. The economy is also closely linked to São Paulo, and its industry is heavily concentrated in agricultural processing for its rich agricultural hinterland. Like Belo Horizonte, Curitiba benefits from industries which are relocating or expanding from São Paulo, including a Volvo plant. Industrial employment accounted for some 20% of the work force.

Porto Alegre is the southernmost of the metropolitan regions, in the state of Rio Grande do Sul. Culturally, it is more similar to Argentina than to Rio or the Northeast. Its resident population was 2,616,051 in 1985. With a labour force of 1,193,686, its labour force participation rate of 58% is comparable to São Paulo's. More than 25% of the occupied work force is in industry, but is less productive than Curitiba, São Paulo or Rio in terms of output per worker. As in Curitiba, industry is heavily concentrated in processing agricultural products, especially meat and leather goods. The proportion of informal activities is very low, with only 23% of employees lacking work cards. Only 14.7% of the labour force earn less than one minimum wage.

Summary

Brazil has grown rapidly in the last century. It has industrialized and urbanized significantly. Regional contrasts are still large, even among the relatively homogenous urban areas. This study focuses on one aspect of the regional differentiation — the determination of wages and regional labour market patterns. The next chapter discusses historical trends in the spatial patterns of Brazil's economic development to provide a context for the regional wage estimates and a basis for interpreting the findings in later chapters.

Notes

1. Martine (1989) on fertility, and Ablas et al (1985) on urbanisation.

2. There is considerable debate over whether this economic growth was or was not really a "miracle." In particular, several authors have argued that the rapid expansion merely utilized excess capacity from the severe government-induced recession of 1964-67.

3. In 1990, the CGT split into two rival organizations.

4. The ten metropolitan regions distinguished in IBGE surveys since the 1970s are Belém, Fortaleza, Recife, Salvador, Belo Horizonte, Rio de Janeiro, São Paulo, Curitiba, Porto Alegre, and the Distrito Federal. The Distrito Federal is not analyzed in this paper because its economy is heavily dependent on the public expenditures associated with the seat of the federal government and hence represents a special noncomparable case. Goiânia which qualified as a metropolitan region after the 1980 census has been excluded because comparable data is not available from the 1970s. The terms city, region, area, and metropolitan region will be used interchangeably in the text to refer to these nine metropolitan regions. In the cases where data by metropolitan region was

unavailable, information was presented by the corresponding states, as for example in Table 3.3.

5. Because income distribution is highly skewed, the median is a more meaningful measure of central tendency. This is especially true for Brazil which has one of the most highly skewed distributions of income in the world. Later analysis will focus on the average of log income which also reduces the weight given to the few very highly-paid individuals in the samples.

6. All figures are in 1985 U.S. dollars unless otherwise noted. In October 1985, the official exchange rate was Cr$7,830/US$1.

7. For example, Rocha (1989) shows that the price level in Belém rose in 1986 as a consequence of more severe food supply problems in that city than elsewhere.

8. Approximately US$50/month.

9. This development pole, begun in 1972, implanted an integrated petrochemical park with infrastructure for private industries which make use of its chemical products. The pole absorbed almost one-third of all public sector investment in the Northeast for several years. It is highly capital intensive. Souza and Araújo (1986) estimate that each of the 17,000 jobs created in the complex by 1979 cost US$200,000 in investment. This compares with a cost of US$38,000 per job in the nearby industrial park of Aratú.

3 Historical trends affecting urban wages

Wage levels differ significantly across Brazil's major urban areas, but so too do the composition of the labour force, the pace of demographic change, the rates of economic growth, and the composition of employment. This chapter presents an overview of historical trends which have affected urban wage levels, whether through relative changes in labour supply, in labour demand, or different institutional developments. The importance of these trends will be addressed in Chapter 9 where the estimated patterns and persistence of regional labour market differences will be analyzed. The discussion here is organized into four broad categories: historical trends in labour supply, labour demand, economic integration, and institutional features of wage determination.

Labour supply: demographics, migration, and education

Other things being equal, an area with more abundant labour will have lower wages if wages are determined by competitive markets. Does the pattern of labour distribution show abundance in low-wage areas? In general, the opposite is true. Labour supply has grown most rapidly in São Paulo both through natural increase and migration whereas the low-wage cities of Fortaleza and Recife have grown relatively more slowly.

Table 3.1
Total population shares by state, 1872-1980

Region/State	1872	1900	1940	1960	1980
North	3.40%	4.00%	3.60%	3.69%	4.94%
Amazonas	-	-	-	1.02%	1.20%
Pará	-	-	-	2.20%	2.86%
Northeast	46.70%	38.70%	35.00%	31.74%	29.28%
Bahia	13.99%	12.15%	9.50%	8.48%	7.96%
Ceará	7.27%	4.87%	5.07%	4.71%	4.45%
Pernambuco	8.47%	6.76%	6.52%	5.85%	5.16%
Southeast	40.50%	44.90%	44.50%	43.47%	43.47%
Minas Gerais	20.54%	20.61%	6.34%	13.89%	11.25%
Rio de Janeiro	10.65%	9.96%	8.76%	9.53%	9.49%
São Paulo	8.43%	13.10%	17.41%	18.37%	21.03%
South	7.30%	10.30%	13.90%	16.88%	15.99%
Panamá	1.28%	1.87%	3.00%	6.11%	6.41%
Rio Grande do Sul	4.38%	6.59%	8.05%	7.72%	6.53%
Centre-West	2.20%	2.10%	3.10%	4.23%	6.34%
Goiás-Distrito	1.61%	1.46%	2.00%	2.95%	4.24%
Federal	0.60%	0.68%	1.05%	1.28%	2.10%
Mato Grosso					
Total (1,000s)	9,931	17,434	41,236	69,806	117,900

Source: Calculated from IBGE Census Data as presented in Ablas and Fava (1985), Vol. I, Table 2.1; and Ablas et al (1985), Vol. II, Table 1.12.

Population

Portuguese colonization originally focused in what is today the northeast region, around Recife in the State of Pernambuco. The colony's wealth and population remained concentrated there for centuries. In Brazil's first census in 1872, the Northeast contained the largest share of the population (some 47%) compared to 40% in the Southeast. The Northeast, however, has steadily lost its population share as a result of growth in other regions as well as net out-migration during the last 100 years.

24

The fastest growing areas since the 1940s continue to be in the frontier states and the dynamic cities (see Table 3.1). For example, Mato Grosso and Goiás doubled their population shares from 1940 to 1980. Amazonas and Pará have also shown rapid growth. Frontier settlement accounts for most of this population growth. Most of the settlers originate from the Northeast and the South.[1] Of the states with large population shares in 1940, only São Paulo grew significantly. Its population share increased from 17% to 21% of the national population. Other major states showed pronounced declines (Minas Gerais, Bahia, Ceará, Pernambuco) or remained stagnant (Rio de Janeiro).

Urbanization

Urbanization between 1950 and 1980 was extremely rapid. In this period, the urban share of the population increased from 36% to 67%. Although the growth of urban population in the 1950s was strongly affected by migration, the pace of urban growth since 1970 has been largely driven by natural increase in the cities themselves, in spite of rapid declines in fertility over the same period.[2] Consequently, by the 1970s, the major migration flows in Brazil were between urban areas, not from rural to urban areas. In 1977, for example, only 16.4% of urban residents had migrated from rural areas, while 28% had come from other urban areas (see Table 3.2). The pace of urban growth was very strong in the country's largest cities, the metropolitan regions. In the 1960s, the metropolitan regions grew more rapidly than the overall population increase of 2.9%. Rio de Janeiro grew 4.1% and São Paulo by 7.0% annually, while the other seven metropolitan regions grew by an average of 5.7% annually.

Table 3.2
Migration in Brazil:
Shares of urban and rural residents by origin, 1977

Area at Birth	Previous Area of Residence		
	Urban	Rural	All
Native	55.4%	72.7%	61.3%
From Elsewhere			
Urban	28.0%	4.9%	20.1%
Rural	16.4%	22.4%	18.5%
No Declaration	0.2%	0.1%	0.1%
All	100.0%	100.0%	100.0%
Total	70,732,393	36,846,523	107,578,916

Source: Author's tabulations from PNAD 1977 data.

Migration

Table 3.3 shows that since 1960, natural increase has dominated migration flows in accounting for state population growth. Paraná's shift from an area of in-migration in the 1960s to an area of out-migration in the 1970s stands out clearly in this table. This was largely a rural phenomena. The same is true of Pará's population growth, which received large inflows in the 1970s in settlement projects. The other net in-migration states, Rio de Janeiro and São Paulo reversed ranking. São Paulo's rate of migratory increase rose from 0.55% to 0.89%, while Rio's in-migration rate fell by half from 0.82% to 0.37% Both of these states are heavily influenced by growth in their respective metropolitan regions.

Table 3.3
Population growth by state: estimates of natural versus migratory increase (%)

State	1960/1970			1970/1980		
	Natural	Migratory	Total	Natural	Migratory	Total
Pará	3.3	0.2	3.5	3.8	0.8	4.6
Bahia	2.8	-0.5	2.3	2.8	-0.4	2.4
Ceará	3.4	-0.5	2.9	2.7	-0.7	2.0
Pernambuco	2.9	-0.5	2.4	2.6	-0.8	1.8
Minas Gerais	2.7	-1.0	1.7	2.0	-0.5	1.5
Rio de Janeiro	2.2	0.8	3.0	1.9	0.4	2.2
São Paulo	3.8	0.6	4.4	2.6	0.9	3.5
Paraná	3.9	1.0	5.0	2.0	-1.0	1.0
Rio Grande do Sul	2.6	-0.5	2.1	1.8	-0.2	1.6

Source: Calculated from IBGE Census Data as presented in Ablas and Fava (1985), Vol. I, Tables 2.8 and 2.9. Totals may not sum exactly due to rounding.

Although migration is not a dominant influence on overall population growth in the metropolitan regions, it can have a significant impact on the labour force since migrants are predominantly of working age. Table 3.4 shows that from 1968 to 1977, some 77,262 men between 16 and 54 years of age annually migrated to the metropolitan regions. That represents roughly a 2.4% gross annual increase among working-age men in these areas.

Table 3.4
Average annual migration to major metropolitan regions
of prime-age males, 25-54 years old, 1968-1977

Metropolitan Region	Migrants	Share of Subgroup	Total Subgroup
Belém	728	1.03%	70,746
Fortaleza	543	0.71%	76,705
Recife	2,672	1.95%	136,929
Salvador	1,012	0.91%	110,780
Belo Horizonte	1,292	1.27%	101,900
Rio de Janeiro	19,962	1.74%	1,147,224
São Paulo	46,448	3.40%	1,365,678
Curitiba	4,159	3.24%	128,530
Porto Alegre	1,298	1.07%	121,520
Total	77,262	2.37%	3,260,012

Note: Figures calculated based on time of residence reported by males between 25 and 54 years of age residing in the metropolitan region in 1977 for less than 10 years.
Source: Author's tabulations from PNAD 1977 data.

The variation between metropolitan regions is also interesting. São Paulo stands out as the largest both in absolute and proportional terms. Between 1968 and 1976, it received on average some 46,448 new arrivals each year, representing a 3.4% annual increase in the population subgroup in addition to its natural increase. Over the same period, Rio de Janeiro received the second largest annual contingent in absolute terms, representing a 1.74% annual increase in its male working age population. Curitiba showed itself to be comparable to São Paulo in terms of the pace of immigration relative to the native subgroup — an annual increase of 3.24% — but has much smaller growth in absolute terms. In the Northeast, the annual increases are smaller, but still significant in comparison with natural increase. In Recife the annual immigration reached almost 2%, while in Salvador and Fortaleza it was 0.9% and 0.7%, respectively.[3]

Migration flows, then, are not overwhelmingly significant relative to natural increase in terms of overall population growth in the metropolitan regions, but they are a significant influence on the labour force. It would be difficult to argue that obstacles to migration account for regional wage gaps in the face of these large flows which are both intra- and inter-regional. Furthermore, these patterns of migration are long-standing, dating at least back to the 1950s.[4] They show a steady and substantial flow of working-age people into the metropolitan regions as a whole, and at a faster pace in São Paulo, Rio de Janeiro, and Curitiba than elsewhere. If anything, the pace of migration may have accelerated due to the rapid decline in transportation costs and the increasing accessibility of information. For example, Meneghetti (1988) measured the increasing mobility of labour by using census data to show that a 10% increase in distance reduced migration by some 18% in 1960, but only by 6% in 1980.

To a large degree, migration appears to flow from low income to high income areas. Graham (1970) showed that states with the highest in-migration in the 1950s had the lowest improvement in relative income per capita, i.e., arguing that the in-flows offset rapid growth in output.[5] Buarque de Holanda Filho (1989) showed that migration flows across states were highly correlated with per capita income differences. Milone (1988) used state data in a regression analysis of out-migration and in-migration and also found that out-migration was negatively related to per-capita income and that in-migration was positively related. Paul Singer (1982) diverges from this line of reasoning, arguing that population concentration is not following the pattern of economic expansion. He notes that the regional patterns of industrial concentration and income are relatively unchanged since 1959, but that population concentration has continued to mount. The results of Chapter 7 show that real wage differences may have disappeared in the last decade as a consequence of increasing economic integration of the labour market, lending support to the other authors. This conclusion, however, depends on the quality of the price comparisons, and therefore, the question of a relationship between migration flows and relative income differences remains unresolved.

Labour 'quality'

Another factor which may affect wages is the 'quality' of the work force. In general, if workers are more productive, it can be profitable for firms to pay them higher wages. If individuals in particular regions are systematically more productive, then such regions could be expected to have higher wages.

One index of the potential productivity embodied in the labour force is its level of educational attainment. Schooling levels differ widely across regions, with the Southeast and the South maintaining higher average educational attainment than the rest of the country. Table 3.5 compares average educational attainment in nine selected states, showing how the levels vary across regions, and how they have converged markedly since 1950. Lam and Levinson (1989) confirm this trend for the population as a whole, showing declining dispersion of educational attainment. This convergence at the broader state and national levels is not readily apparent in the metropolitan regions. State educational levels increasing toward Rio's high levels may reflect the rapid pace of urbanization in these cities and hence the greater share of state population with access to schooling.

For the metropolitan regions themselves, Almeida and Barros (1989) show fairly stable educational averages in the nine major metropolitan regions over an entire decade. One probable interpretation is that northeastern migrants to the Southeast are more highly educated than those in their place of origin, but are less educated than those in their place of destination. Hence, the averages could remain the same in all of the areas due to the countervailing influence of shifting population. This hypothesis finds support in Schmertmann (1988) which shows consistent self-selection of migrants to Metropolitan Regions, revealing higher earnings potential (due presumably to unobserved characteristics) than control subgroups.

Table 3.5
Educational attainment by selected states

Mean years of study for population over 5 years old			
State	1950	1980	Change
Pará	1.06	2.54	139.6%
Ceará	0.38	1.94	410.5%
Pernambuco	0.56	2.44	335.7%
Bahia	0.55	1.90	245.5%
Minas Gerais	1.00	3.18	218.0%
Rio de Janeiro	2.66	4.66	75.2%
São Paulo	1.86	4.21	126.3%
Paraná	1.09	3.20	193.6%
Rio Grande do Sul	1.67	4.13	147.3%
Standard Deviation	0.70	0.96	
Relative Education Levels (Rio de Janeiro = 1.00)			
Pará	0.40	0.55	
Ceará	0.14	0.42	
Pernambuco	0.21	0.52	
Bahia	0.21	0.41	
Minas Gerais	0.38	0.68	
Rio de Janeiro	1.00	1.00	
São Paulo	0.70	0.90	
Paraná	0.41	0.69	
Rio Grande do Sul	0.63	0.89	
Coefficient of Variation	0.58	0.31	

Source: Calculated from IBGE Demographic Census 1950 and 1980.

To summarize the historical trends in labour supply, then, São Paulo is the fastest growing area. In addition, large migration flows have a significant impact on labour force growth in metropolitan regions even if they are less relevant to total population increase. Educational levels vary systematically across regions and may influence wage levels. These educational differences appear to have converged substantially through the past three decades. In Chapter 5, regional wage differentials will be estimated in ways which consider potential composition effects in terms of education, and Chapter 6 will test the sensitivity of the results to the inclusion of information about migrants.

Labour demand: spatial patterns of economic activity and productivity

Labour demand may also vary across regions and affect regional wage levels. The availability of complementary factors of production which are region-specific will influence the profitability of expanding employment even with higher pay, and this can positively affect local wages. Additionally, to the degree that it is cheaper to expand production in established areas, regions which produce goods for fast-growing local markets will have a relatively faster pace of demand growth than others.

Unlike other Latin American countries, Brazil appears to have a relatively diversified spatial distribution of economic activity.[6] Even in large countries like Argentina and Mexico, the capital city dominates the country in every respect, while secondary cities are decidedly smaller in population and economic activity. Although São Paulo dominates Brazil, numerous other cities have historically played a central role (Recife, Salvador, and Rio de Janeiro); Brazil's federal government is seated in Brasília; and much of the federal government's employment remains in Rio de Janeiro which also rivals São Paulo in terms of population (with 10 million and 15 million residents, respectively).

Nevertheless, since the 1930s São Paulo has remained clearly ascendant in terms of economic activity, industry, and population growth. It surpassed Rio de Janeiro in population at the turn of the century. In terms of shares of national industrial production, São Paulo surpassed Rio in the 1920s (Table 3.6). Since 1950, São Paulo continues to produce over half of Brazil's industrial output. Rio's share of national industrial production, by contrast, has declined steadily from 20% in 1949 to a little over 10% in 1980.

Table 3.6
Share of industrial value by region and selected states

	1907	1919	1939	1959	1970	1980
North	4.3%	1.3%	1.1%	1.1%	1.0%	2.6%
Northeast	16.7%	16.1%	10.4%	7.6%	5.8%	8.1%
Bahia	3.4%	2.8%	1.4%	2.4%	1.5%	3.6%
Pernambuco	7.4%	6.8%	4.8%	2.6%	2.1%	1.9%
Southeast	58.2%	66.0%	74.3%	78.1%	80.3%	72.2%
Minas Gerais	4.4%	5.6%	6.5%	6.1%	7.1%	8.2%
Rio de	37.6%	28.2%	22.0%	17.3%	15.5%	10.4%
Janeiro	15.9%	31.5%	45.4%	54.5%	57.2%	52.4%
São Paulo						
South	19.9%	16.2%	13.8%	12.4%	12.0%	15.7%
Centre West	0.9%	0.4%	0.4%	0.7%	0.8%	1.4%
Brazil	100.0%	100.0%	100.0%	100.0%	100.0%	100.0%

Source: IBGE Industrial Census, various years.

Industrial concentration

Overall, industrial production became more concentrated in São Paulo from 1920 to 1970, with only a small shift toward decentralization in the 1970s. The North increased its share in the 1970s, largely due to the establishment of a free trade export zone in Manaus. The Northeast also reversed a long-standing declining share with the expansion of industrial output concentrated in Bahia (see Table 3.6). Again, public policy may have been instrumental to this change since the federal government spent billions of dollars in the construction of a petrochemical pole outside of Salvador in the 1970s. Minas Gerais showed a slight increase in its share of output, benefiting from metallurgical, steel, and mechanical plants which are closely integrated with São Paulo's industrial park. Finally, the South and the Centre West showed some expansion, largely based on food processing industries linked to their focus on agricultural production including beef, soy, oranges for orange concentrate, and leather goods.

Overall, industrial firms operate in highly concentrated markets. In 1980, 100 firms accounted for one-third of domestic industrial production, and the top 500 accounted for a little over one-half. Four firms accounted for more than 50% of the market in 46% of the 191 four-digit industrial

33

sectors studied by Willmore (1987), whereas in 76% of these sectors the largest four firms accounted for more than 30% of the market. Again, a majority of these firms operate in São Paulo or have their headquarters there. Even going beyond industrial activities, almost half of the country's 'Top 500' firms are headquartered in São Paulo — including construction, industry, public enterprises, agribusiness, and services, alike.[7]

Labour productivity

Jobs differ with respect to their productivity. Equally skilled workers, when placed in different factories, will differ in terms of productivity whenever technology, organization, capitalization, management, and other factors vary. The degree of these productivity differences can be suggested by measuring labour productivity. More highly capitalized regions, or those benefitting from agglomeration economies will show higher productivity for comparable workers than those without. Hansen (1989) shows that firms located closer to the centre of Greater São Paulo have higher labour productivity than those located farther away in the state. Labour productivity also varies sharply across regions (Table 3.7).

The state of São Paulo has the largest number of workers in manufacturing and consistently maintains high productivity relative to the national average and to the other states. The state of Rio de Janeiro also maintains a high ranking in productivity of manufacturing. The states of the North and Northeast — Pará, Ceará, and Pernambuco — are among the least productive. The key exception to this pattern is Bahia which experienced enormous industrial expansion in the 1970s, doubling industrial employment and increasing the value of output at a rate three times faster than the national average. Consequently, by 1980, Bahia appears to be the state with the highest productivity. This high productivity, however, pertains to a small segment of the labour force (about 10%, see Table 2.2) while the high productivity in São Paulo's industry affects almost one-third of its work force.

Table 3.7
Labour productivity in manufacturing by selected states

State	1950		1970		1980	
	Workers Per Firm	Output Per Worker	Workers Per Firm	Output Per Worker	Workers Per Firm	Output Per Worker
Pará	11	53	12	20	21	986
Ceará	6	56	13	28	33	904
Pernambuco	21	64	15	30	30	1,524
Bahia	7	49	7	34	26	3,037
Minas Gerais	8	87	11	45	35	2,216
Rio de Janeiro	24	105	26	49	41	2,151
São Paulo	19	114	26	51	49	2,252
Paraná	8	115	11	38	28	2,199
Rio Grande do Sul	7	107	12	36	51	1,571
Brazil	14	42	16	44	39	2,019

Notes: Value of output in 1,000s of Cruzeiros. A currency reform in the 1960s of 1:1000 and inflation affect intertemporal comparisons.
Source: IBGE Censo Industrial 1950, 1970, and 1980.

Although this study is not directly concerned with labour outside the metropolitan regions, it is important to note that productivity in the agricultural sector varies across regions in ways which are highly correlated with the productivity differences in industry. Table 3.8 shows that the state of São Paulo has markedly higher levels of agricultural productivity than any other state. Paraná and Rio Grande do Sul are next in line in terms of rural productivity, while Ceará and Pernambuco have extremely low productivity levels. If regional differences in productivity are an important contributor to urban wage differences, then the rural differences would have similar ranks and larger magnitudes than the urban differences.

Table 3.8
Rural share of population and productivity by selected states
(population over 14 years old)

State	Rural Share of Population	Value Added per Worker 1975	1980
Maranhão	64.0%	15.72	18.12
Ceará	42.8%	18.94	22.76
Pernambuco	30.7%	25.73	28.37
Bahia	44.8%	27.81	34.12
Minas Gerais	27.6%	53.96	60.18
Rio de Janeiro	6.8%	77.22	76.16
São Paulo	7.8%	100.84	109.22
Paraná	32.2%	85.08	84.62
Rio Grande do Sul	31.2%	87.88	105.15

Notes: Value added per worker measured in thousands of 1980 cruzeiros. In 1980, the official exchange rate was Cr$50/US$.
Sources: Rural shares of population from author's tabulations using the IBGE's PNAD 1985 data. Value added per worker from Rodolfo Hoffman, coordinator (1990), and calculated from the IBGE's Agricultural Census Data.

Transaction costs and increasing economic integration

In addition to spatial differences in local demand and supply conditions, the ease of interregional communication, factor movements, and trade should affect labour market differences over time. In fact, the pace of economic integration in Brazil has been extremely rapid in the last few decades, leading scholars to predict a convergence of regional wage differences (Pfefferman and Webb 1983, Morley 1983).

Brazil is a country of continental dimensions, but until recently its infrastructure was restricted to the large population centres along its coast. Since 1950, however, a network of communications and transportation has expanded to incorporate the entire territory, including some of the farthest reaches of the Amazon. From 1960 to 1980, the kilometers of roadway in

Brazil increased by 200%; the bus fleet grew 1622%, and the number of telephones installed increased by 669% (Meneghetti 1988).

Commerce has steadily expanded as a share of total economic activity. Interstate trade tripled from 1943 to 1961, and then increased about ten-fold in the next 20 years (Ablas and Fava 1985). As a share of GDP, interstate commerce grew from 16% in 1947 to 33.5% in 1976 (Ablas and Fava 1985). This increase occurred at a time when total GDP was growing at an average annual pace of almost 7%. The degree of product market integration can be inferred from the presence of manufactured products in the farthest reaches of the frontier, at prices which differ little between frontier outposts but which incorporate transportation costs (Almeida 1992).

The major flows of interstate trade are dominated by the Southeast (see Figure 3.1). Some 30% of interstate trade is among the four states of the Southeast region. In every other region, trade with the Southeast dominates intra-regional trade, as can be seen in Figure 3.1. For example, commerce in the Northeast was largely intra-regional in the 1940s — with Cr$1.4 billion of trade within the Northeast compared to Cr$245 million with the Southeast. By 1969, however, intra-regional trade was Cr$1.9 trillion — some 30% less than trade with the Southeast which had climbed to Cr$2.9 trillion (Ablas and Fava 1985).

Government incentives which aimed to redirect investment toward the relatively undeveloped Northeast and frontiers, along with a rapid expansion in financial institutions in the main centres, also led to an effective integration of capital markets across Brazil in the 1960s (Guimarães Neto 1984). Thus, the economy which was characterized in the early 1960s by Baer as an 'archipelago of island economies' is today frequently discussed as a dynamic well-integrated economy.

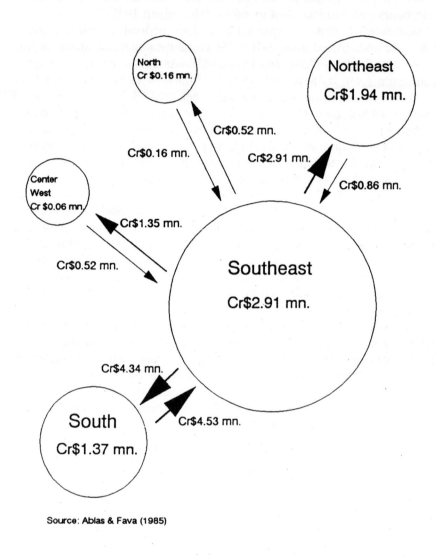

Source: Ablas & Fava (1985)

Figure 3.1 Major flows of interstate trade, 1969

Public policy and institutions of wage determination

Brazil has unique institutions and political processes which also influence wages. Three particular aspects will be discussed in terms of their possible contribution to observed wage differentials: government wage policy, union activity, and firm-level pay and employment practices.

Government wage policy

Government wage policy over the past three decades has operated in ways which would, if anything, lead regional wage levels to converge. When the minimum wage was first established in 1940, it was set at different levels for different regions. The highest minimum wage was always set for the cities of São Paulo and Rio de Janeiro, with lower minima established for smaller cities. Beginning in the 1960s, however, the number of separate categories were gradually diminished until 1984 when a single unified national minimum wage was established.

There is a good deal of debate over the effect of the minimum wage on wage levels in Brazil.[8] For the purposes of this study, however, it is clear that the regional differentiation of the minimum wage cannot realistically explain the continued divergence of regional wage levels, given that regional wage differences persisted throughout a period during which the minimum wages were gradually unified.

Another feature of government wage policy, indexation, could account for some of the persistence in regional wage differentials. Since 1964, the government has mandated that workers be compensated for wages eroded by inflation according to a single national index of inflation. Until 1979, the index used to adjust wages was based in part on a consumer price survey for Rio de Janeiro given that price surveys were not conducted in other places. Hence, a certain uniformity in wage adjustments from year to year was imposed on all formal wage contracts. The importance of this may be very great given that inflation has been quite high — 30% to 60% in the 1960s and over 100% annually through most of the 1980s. If all nominal wages are adjusted in such large discrete jumps, the ability of market conditions or other factors to bring about a convergence in wages across regions may be diminished. On the other hand, firms and workers have a variety of means to circumvent mandated wage adjustments (whether establishing floors or limits) and in this regard, the government wage policy may be unimportant to the issue of regional wage differentials.

Unions

Union activity varies strongly across regions and could contribute to regional wage differences. In particular, unions are strongest and most active in São Paulo. Brazil's largest firms, many of which operate in highly concentrated markets, are also located or headquartered in São Paulo. A region like São Paulo, with a disproportionate share of the nation's large firms operating in concentrated markets, may have rents which can be claimed by workers through negotiation and bargaining — especially when the workers are highly concentrated and organized. This is nowhere more apparent than in the industrial suburbs where virtually the entire automobile industry is focused and the nation's strongest metallurgical union is located. Union activity, however, has been highly variable over time as a result of political change and military repression and is therefore unlikely to explain the long-standing regional wage differences.

Behaviour of firms

Firm level strategies may have changed over time in Brazil in ways that would significantly affect regional wage differences. Although regional differences in employment, work, and pay practices are widely discussed in Brazil, there is little direct comparative evidence.[9] Employment is generally characterized by high turnover, low pay, and quick training periods, indicating a fairly homogeneous and active competitive labour market. On the other hand, some studies have found significant subgroups for whom pay and employment may be strongly affected by organizational and institutional practices. Morley (1979) found significant numbers of large firms who operate like internal labour markets — paying competitive wages for entry-level positions but attempting to insulate their work force through internal promotion. Schmitz (1985) found cases where wages were not directly attributable to worker skills but rather were set to ensure high levels of worker motivation, especially when costly equipment or continuous production processes were involved. From interviews, the range of pay and employment practices in Rio and Recife appeared to be quite large. Some employers treated workers as mere material inputs and spoke of workers disparagingly, while others had adopted 'personnel management' techniques and spoke about links between wages, promotions, motivation, and productivity. Whether these employment practices differ systematically across regions, and whether or not they contribute to regional wage differentials, there is even less evidence available upon how such practices may have changed over time. The potential impact of firm-level differences

40

in pay and employment practices upon regional wage differences will be raised again and evaluated in Chapters 5 and 9.

Summary

Various historical trends may have a bearing on regional wage differences and labour markets. All of Brazil's regions have experienced rapid population growth and significant migration, but São Paulo stands out as the fastest growing in terms of labour force growth. Educational levels are very different across the major cities, but they appear to have converged in recent decades. Productivity differentials do not appear to have changed markedly over the last four decades, with the exception of a steep improvement in Salvador beginning in the 1970s. The country's economic integration has proceeded very rapidly since the 1950s in physical and organizational terms. Government policy has also acted to encourage national homogeneity in the labour market through nationwide indexation and unification of the various local minimum wages. Union activity varies strongly across regions, but the level of labour mobilization has been seriously affected by national policy and repression. Finally, employment and pay practices may differ substantially across regions, but historical data on trends are unavailable.

The next four chapters will analyze regional wage differentials from a static perspective, but the historical trends discussed here will provide an important basis for a final evaluation of regional wage disparities in Chapters 9 and 10.

Notes

1. Paraná was the site of massive expulsion of rural workers in the 1970s as a consequence of the expansion of soy cultivation. See George Martine 1982, 'Expansão e Retração de Emprego na Fronteira Agrícola', *Revista de Economía Política*, No. 7, pp. 53-76.

2. Martine (1989) on fertility, and Ablas et al (1985) on urbanisation.

3. These annual numbers of immigrants were calculated by taking the number of individuals who reported immigrating from outside the *state* between 1 and 9 years before and dividing it by 9. The figures therefore underestimate the amount of annual immigration in two ways. First, they exclude those who immigrated in the last year, a figure which was generally three or four times higher than the annual numbers. Thus, these estimates exclude what may be a significant amount of short-term (less than one year) migration. Secondly, it excludes intra-state migration which may account for a substantial part of movement to the metropolitan regions, especially in populous states like São Paulo.

4. Sahota, G.S. 1968, 'An Economic Analysis of Internal Migration in Brazil,' *Journal of Political Economy*, 76(2).

5. As cited in Graham and Merrick (1979), p.135.

6. Colombia is another exception in this regard.

7. In 1989, 44% of the "Top 500" firms were headquartered in São Paulo and this share had increased steadily during the 1980s (see *Conjuntura Econômica*, August 1989).

8. See, for example, Souza and Baltar (1983), Taylor (1980), and Velloso (1990).

9. Schmitz (1985) does compare firms in several distinct regions, but the focus is on technological differences among firms rather than regional differences.

4 Estimating regional wage differentials: Methods, assumptions and sample selection

This chapter specifies the econometric methods used to investigate whether regional wage differences are a result of compositional differences. It discusses choices made concerning the relevant sample of individuals and the specification of four earnings equations used in the analysis. The following chapter will present the findings from the application of this methodology to a Brazilian household survey conducted in 1985.

What is 'regional' about a wage differential?

The methodology presented here is an effort to find out how much of the wage distribution in Brazil is attributable to region-specific factors. 'Region-specific factors', however, may be defined in various ways. Immobile natural resources are clearly region-specific. The social organization and people who reside in a particular region, however, are also arguably region-specific since it is impossible to completely relocate an entire city of people and expect them to function as before. In this sense, a simple comparison of average wages from one region to another does show the existing 'regional wage differential'. This would be measured as an unconditional wage difference between regions.

Such a broad definition simplifies the degree of mobility into and out of regions, as well as the compositional differences which may not be immutable aspects of a region. Since individuals can and do migrate, it may be useful to define region-specific factors as the entire context faced by an individual when moving from one place to another. In this case, the regional wage differential would seek to indicate how much income a marginal individual would gain (or lose) in moving from one region to the next. If workers are heterogeneous, the wage difference could be measured for a marginal individual within a group of comparable workers — the result of calculating the regional wage differential conditional on personal characteristics. The wage differential measured in this way would reflect differences in region-wide productivity or different kinds of jobs available. In this way, the kinds of jobs and the productivity associated with the particular composition of economic activities in a region would be considered 'region-specific'.

If one takes the above process one step further, however, the jobs themselves can be considered 'movable'. If a wage difference conditional on personal characteristics were the result of a more highly productive industrial job which could be easily moved to an area with more abundant workers, then the job is not really a 'region-specific factor' and the measured wage differential is a job-related differential, not a regional one. There is no clear boundary, however, between 'region-specific' and 'fully mobile' jobs. A wage differential across regions between workers in comparable occupations and sectors could indicate important region-specific productivity differences within these occupations and sectors. A wage differential of this kind would be measured conditional on job characteristics.

In addition, local economies have important internal interdependencies which make it impossible to simply decompose and reallocate sectors and occupations. There are important interactions between the quality of the local labour force and the kinds and numbers of jobs generated by a local economy. It is the productivity in the interstices of the local economic matrix — composed of people *and* jobs — which is perhaps the most appropriate focus for an analysis of regional wage differences. Such a differential would relate to the workings of the entire local economic complex, and not to any decomposable, removable, and movable element of it. To the degree that it is possible to measure wage differentials conditional on personal and job characteristics, then, it is possible to measure this kind of differential inherent in the functioning of the local economy.

In sum, the simple average wage difference across regions is unsatisfying because it ignores compositional differences between regions. The wage difference conditional on personal characteristics does indicate an important difference between regions — but it would remain unclear whether such a differential is associated with distinct and spatially mobile job opportunities or with the functioning of the local economy as a whole. A wage difference conditional on job characteristics alone would make it impossible to distinguish that part of the measured difference attributable to heterogeneity of individuals and that part attributable, again, to productivity levels inherent in the particular organization of the local economy. Finally, a wage difference conditional on job and personal characteristics measures factors which may be more clearly considered region-specific, i.e., those factors which inhere in the interaction and functioning of the regional economy.

In any event, estimates of wage differentials in all four categories (unconditional, conditional on personal characteristics, conditional on job characteristics, or conditional on job and personal characteristics) contain important information about the regional economy. This may be least intuitive in the case of the wage differences conditional on personal characteristics since it appears to say nothing about region-specific factors but only about the kinds of people who 'happen' to reside in an area. Labour force quality, however, is 'region-specific' to the degree that it depends on the local provision and quality of education, as well as the kinds, quantities, and quality of job training locally available.[1] This may be equally true for the kinds of jobs and sectors of economic activity which are located in any particular location. The automobile industry could have been established in Rio or Salvador, but it wasn't. Now that it has been established in São Paulo, it influences the development of other related firms in its area.

The estimated wage differential between regions conditional on job and personal characteristics is the most interesting for the purposes of this study because it measures productivity which inheres in the regional economy independently of composition effects due to workers or jobs. Nevertheless, the other measures provide valuable data for interpreting differences in pay across regions.

Estimation and assumptions

The econometric techniques employed to evaluate the regional wage differences follow the scheme outlined above. The core of the methodology is an earnings function which regresses log wages on dummy variables for metropolitan regions, using other variables of personal characteristics and job structure as controls. The mean difference in wages between regions is calculated for the entire sample, as well as the wage difference conditional on personal characteristics, on job characteristics, and on the two sets of characteristics combined.

The dummy variables are used to capture the average differences between individuals' earnings in the different metropolitan areas, before and after adjustments are made for observed factors which may affect earnings. If wage determination were taking place in a national labour market with workers and jobs randomly distributed in spatial terms, then geographic dispersion should not have any predictive power on wages — unless it exists as compensation for nonmonetary aspects of job-related or residence-related quality of life (see Chapter 7), or if it is systematically correlated with unobserved productivity differences. The main hypothesis to be tested is whether the coefficients on regional dummy variables, conditional on the observed factors, are zero. If they are different from zero, then explanation must be sought in sample bias, excluded variables or unobserved characteristics, compensating differentials, market disequilibria, regional segmentation, or region-specific productivity.

Consider log wages (ϖ) to be a linear function of place of residence ($\mathbf{R}$), observed factors ($\mathbf{X}$), unobserved factors ($\mathbf{U}$), and an orthogonal error term (ϵ_0), as

$$\varpi_i = \mathbf{R}_i \rho + \mathbf{X}_i \chi + \mathbf{U}_i \mu + \epsilon_{0i}. \tag{4.1}$$

The objective is to estimate the difference in wages attributable to place of residence (ρ). If place of residence were uncorrelated with all observed and unobserved factors ($\mathbf{R'X}=0$ and $\mathbf{R'U}=0$), then an easily interpreted and unbiased estimate of ρ could be obtained with the following regression:

$$\varpi_i = \mathbf{R}_i \rho + \epsilon_{1i}, \tag{4.2}$$

where ϵ_{1i} is an orthogonal term equal to $\mathbf{X}_i \chi + \mathbf{U}_i \mu + \epsilon_{0i}$. Place of residence, however, is correlated with other factors ($\mathbf{R'X} \neq 0$ or $\mathbf{R'U} \neq 0$). If there are regional influences on wages which are independent of the left-out variables, then this correlation can lead to biased estimates in regression (4.2) for ρ. To the degree that the left-out variables are functions of place of residence, ρ will still provide an accurate estimate for the impact of region-specific factors.

It is useful to consider particular variables for which this issue is important. For example, education is frequently used as a proxy for acquired skills and is positively correlated with earnings in general. Hence wherever place of residence is positively correlated with education, regression (4.2) will attribute the impact of education to that portion of log earnings variance which is correlated with place of residence. That is, the expected wage in a region with systematically higher education levels will be greater than the expected wage in that region conditional on education.

A similar result would be obtained by excluding age. In general, earnings are lower for populations with smaller proportions of prime age workers. This relationship is given content by positing an impact of accumulated experience on an individual's earnings. Therefore, regression (4.2) would overestimate ρ whenever a region has a higher proportion of prime age workers and age has a positive impact on earnings. Head of Household

46

status is a third personal characteristics which should be considered since it indicates an individual's labour force attachment. The term 'head of household' is a social definition, referring to individuals who are expected to provide the household's primary source of income.[2] Because of this expectation, such individuals are in the labour force more regularly, accumulating job experience, and may therefore be more productive than individuals less committed to the labour market. Consequently, populations with a larger share of heads of households would be expected to have higher earnings on average than populations with lower shares. This would lead regression (4.2) again, to overestimate the regional wage differential (ρ) in regions with higher than average shares of heads of households. Note that if the positive relationship between region and the left-out variable is a structural relationship (e.g., with the place of residence being in some sense the 'cause' of the population's higher educational level), then the interpretation of the coefficient on the regional variables would remain unaffected because it measures a regional impact on earnings, even if the relationship is an indirect one.[3]

To address the possibility that these personal characteristics — education, age, and household status — are not region-specific, but rather inhere in individuals who are mobile within the labour market, the following regression can be estimated:

$$\varpi_i = \mathbf{R}_i \, \rho + \mathbf{PC}_i \, \varphi + \epsilon_{2i} \qquad (4.3)$$

where **PC** is a matrix of variables representing an individual's level of education, age, and head of household status and ϵ_{2i} is an error term equal to $\mathbf{U}_i \, \mu + \epsilon_{0i}$. Job characteristics are not included in this case because they are assumed either to have no meaningful[4] impact on wages or to be region-specific. This regression will provide accurate estimates for regional wage differences if such differences are independent of personal characteristics; personal characteristics are uncorrelated with other unobserved variables; and job characteristics are region-specific.

Whether or not jobs are region-specific, there is ample evidence that workers' wages are strongly influenced by where they work and what they do. Furthermore, if there are regional wage differences, it would very useful to know whether they can be largely attributed to the jobs available in different areas or if the differences come from some other source. Other studies of regional wage differentials have paid little attention to the impact of job characteristics. For example, Fields and Schultz (1980) studied regional wage differentials in Colombia, emphasizing only the observed and unobserved variation among individuals and place of residence. They considered urban/rural differences, which could be considered a proxy for productivity differentials between agricultural and nonagricultural sectors. Nevertheless, the composition of employment between urban areas and levels of capitalization across these sectors could be significant, creating a bias in their analysis due to left-out variables. Heckman and Hotz (1986) analyzed Panamanian household survey data with standard 'human capital' specifications, but qualified their findings by recognizing the limitations of excluding sectoral factors. They concluded that their results were consistent with hypotheses of sectoral segmentation, although they remained skeptical of this hypothesis given that the findings were also consistent with alternative and more conventional explanations. An estimation which includes job characteristics, then, could directly confront the possibility that regional wage differentials reflect regional variations in employment patterns.

Variables representing job characteristics can be used to capture some of the systematic variation in earnings opportunities across regions which are apparent in Brazil along many dimensions — formal vs. informal (Barros 1988), Internal labour markets (Morley 1979), private vs. public (Macedo 1986), technique of production (Schmitz 1985), and by industry (Menezes 1988). In the author's interviews with managers, negotiators, and union leaders in Rio de Janeiro and Recife, these agents indicated that they are themselves aware of such segmentation of opportunity: primarily between small firms which have short promotion ladders and little latitude for paying much more than negotiated wage floors, and larger 'dynamic' firms which pay premia over the negotiated settlements to ensure stability in their labour force and to reduce intra-firm tension. In addition, all those interviewed discussed market conditions only in the context of particular well-defined categories. That is, agents referred to market conditions for particular occupational, sectoral and geographical subgroups of the working population, and not for the labour force as a whole.[5]

The composition of jobs offered by a region may be more problematic for estimation of wage differentials than the composition of the work force (in terms of age, education, and household status) for a variety of reasons. In Brazil, these features do vary across regions in highly stable ways. Capital has not shown itself to be particularly mobile. Brazil's spatial pattern of industrial location and productivity has remained relatively unchanged for more than 30 years (see Chapter 3). In the cities of the Northeast, evidence shows that despite rapid paces of industrialization these cities have been unable to change the composition of the jobs they offer or to increase the number of jobs sufficiently to change the overall employment pattern (Kon 1989, Jatobá 1986, Gomes et al 1985). Firms frequently report they are interested in hiring workers who are trainable rather than workers who are already trained,[6] indicating the importance of specific skills and jobs in pay

48

determination. Variation in capitalization is also evident across firms, which could significantly affect marginal productivity from one employer to another (Menezes 1988). Econometric studies have shown that job characteristics alone, i.e., sector and occupation, can account for large proportions of variance in log earnings (Medeiros 1982). In such an event, the appropriate model may be one which sees wages deriving from jobs with particular effects on productivity and pay.

Assuming that job characteristics are key to wage determination, and that personal characteristics are independent of the regional wage differences, the following equation could be estimated:

$$\varpi_i = \mathbf{R}_i \, \rho + \mathbf{JC}_i \, \gamma + \epsilon_{3i}, \qquad (4.4)$$

where ρ captures any systematic wage differences between regions which are not captured by the job characteristic variables ($\mathbf{JC}$). Once again, the error term ϵ_{3i} includes errors due to the exclusion of unobserved variables ($\mathbf{U}$) and the true orthogonal error term (ϵ_{0i}). The personal characteristic variables are excluded because they are assumed either to be orthogonal to the effects of place of residence and job characteristics on wages or to be themselves dependent on place of residence. Under the assumptions that residence and job characteristics are uncorrelated with unobserved productive factors ($\mathbf{R'U} = \mathbf{JC'U} = 0$) and personal characteristics are not a meaningful factor in regional wage differentiation, then the estimates of regional wage differentials from regression (4.4) will be preferable to estimates from regressions (4.2) and (4.3).

Estimating regional wage differentials with the inclusion of job characteristic variables alone, however, has its problems. First, it ignores the differing composition of individuals by personal characteristics which may not be region-specific. Second, all jobs are not entirely mobile and hence some of the wage variation attributed to the job may be more properly construed as region-specific.

If wages were determined by the conjunction of personal and job characteristics and these factors were not region-specific, then the above regressions (4.2), (4.3), and (4.4) will overestimate the regional wage differences. Assuming that the process by which individuals get jobs is stochastically independent of the process determining wages, that choice of location is also stochastically independent of the wage process, and that returns to included factors are the same in all regions, the proper specification would be:

$$\varpi_i = \mathbf{R}_i \, \rho + \mathbf{PC}_i \, \varphi + \mathbf{JC}_i \, \gamma + \epsilon_{4i}. \qquad (4.5)$$

49

In this case, the error term includes only unobserved variables and the true orthogonal error term. Again, the correlation of personal and job characteristics with unobserved variables would affect the estimates of ρ, φ, and γ. So long as place of residence (**R**) is uncorrelated with the unobserved variables and is correlated with observed personal and job characteristics, regression (4.5) will provide a lower bound estimate of wage differences caused by region-specific factors, i.e., it assumes that wage differences attributable to personal and job characteristics are not region-specific.

In sum, the following equations were estimated:

$$\varpi_i = \alpha_1 + \mathbf{R}_i\, \rho_1 + \epsilon_{1i} \tag{4.6}$$

$$\varpi_i = \alpha_2 + \mathbf{R}_i\, \rho_2 + \mathbf{PC}_i\, \varphi_2 + \epsilon_{2i} \tag{4.7}$$

$$\varpi_i = \alpha_3 + \mathbf{R}_i\, \rho_3 + \mathbf{JC}_i\, \gamma_3 + \epsilon_{3i} \tag{4.8}$$

$$\varpi_i = \alpha_4 + \mathbf{R}_i\, \rho_4 + \mathbf{PC}_i\, \varphi_4 + \mathbf{JC}_i\, \gamma_4 + \epsilon_{4i} \tag{4.9}$$

where:

ϖ = log hourly wage;

α = constant term;

R = an eight-column matrix of dummy variables for metropolitan region;

PC = a vector of variables representing personal characteristics: four dummy variables for educational categories, five for age categories, and one for head of household status;

JC = a vector of variables representing the individual's job characteristics: nine dummies for occupational categories, eight for sector of activity, and 1 to distinguish employees from the self-employed;

φ, γ, and ρ = vectors of associated coefficients; and

ϵ = error term, assumed to be orthogonal to included variables.

The definitions for these variables are presented in Table 4.1.

Table 4.1
Variables used in the regression analysis

Categories for Years of Schooling Completed:
EST0	Less than one year
EST1	1 to 4 years
EST2	5 to 8 years
EST3	9 to 11 years
EST4	12 and more years

Categories for Age Groups:
IDA1	15 to 24 years
IDA2	25 to 34 years
IDA3	35 to 44 years
IDA4	45 to 54 years
IDA5	55 to 64 years
IDA6	65 years and older

Head of Household Status:
CHEFE 1 if individual is considered head of household
        0 otherwise

Employment Status:
  EMPL 1 if individual is an employee
        0 if an individual is self-employed

Occupational Categories:
OCC0	Miscellaneous	
OCC1	Administrative	All managers and directors.
OCC2	Professional	Professions requiring extensive training and involving high degree of autonomy
OCC3	Technical	Occupations requiring technical training but with less autonomy
OCC4	Clerical	Office work, support staff, messengers, etc.
OCC5	High Skill Production	Production work requiring extensive training and some autonomy of decision-making
OCC6	Low Skill Production	Production work involving moderate training and routine tasks
OCC7	Transportation	Drivers, Pilots, and engineers
OCC8	Sales	Retail sales personnel
OCC9	Personal Services	All personal services: domestic, barbers, waiters, etc.

51

Sectoral Categories:

RAM1	Heavy Industry	Metallurgy, Chemicals, Vehicles, ...
RAM2	Light Industry	Furniture, Textiles, Leather goods, ...
RAM3	Construction	Construction
RAM4	Commerce	Wholesale, Retail, etc...
RAM5	Transportation	Road, Maritime, Air, ...
RAM6	Finance	Banking, insurance, ...
RAM7	Services	Restaurants, Tourism, Barbers, Domestics, ...
RAM8	Public Administration	Direct public administration

The coefficient on the dummy variable for a particular metropolitan region, ρ, represents a point estimate of the expected wage gain (or loss) for moving from the excluded region to that region, conditional on the other variables as discussed above. Define the difference in the log of real wages between region k and the excluded region j to be, $\hat{\omega}_k$ as

$$\hat{\omega}_k = \omega_k - \omega_j$$

Under the assumption of orthogonality in the error term, the associated estimates can be interpreted as conditional expectations as follows:

$$E(\rho_{1k}) = E(\hat{\omega}_k) \tag{4.10}$$

$$E(\rho_{2k}) = E(\hat{\omega}_k | \mathbf{PC}) \tag{4.11}$$

$$E(\rho_{3k}) = E(\hat{\omega}_k | \mathbf{JC}), \text{ and} \tag{4.12}$$

$$E(\rho_{4k}) = E(\hat{\omega}_k | \mathbf{PC}, \mathbf{JC}). \tag{4.13}$$

Again, this interpretation depends upon the assumptions regarding independence of selection processes and wages, as well as the assumption of a single national market in the sense that returns to personal and job characteristics are constrained to be equal in all regions. If the model is correctly specified, the metropolitan region coefficients capture the level differences between earnings in different regions.

The objective, then, is to test the hypothesis that the labour markets in the nine metropolitan regions are nationally integrated. If they were fully integrated, comparable workers in comparable jobs would be earning similar wages. Otherwise, the wage differential might be eliminated by arbitrage: with workers moving to higher wage cities; firms relocating to lower wage cities; and/or specialization in labour-intensive products in low wage areas. Furthermore, national integration of these labour markets would ensure that returns to education and experience, as well as marginal productivity in comparable jobs, would all be equal. by constraining all coefficients to be the same, i.e., slopes are all equal across regions, regressions (4.7) through

(4.9), become models for testing national integration under the assumptions of orthogonality discussed above. Under the hypothesis of national integration, the expectation of ρ is zero for all regions. The hypothesis that any particular region is integrated with the excluded city can be tested by using a t-test on ρ_k; while the hypothesis of national integration for all metropolitan regions can be tested with an F-test on the vector of coefficients, ρ.

The sample and selection problems

The data analyzed are from the *Pesquisa Nacional de Amostra de Domicílios* (PNAD), a household survey collected by the *Instituto Brasileiro de Geografía e Estatísticas* (IBGE) in October of each year, using sampling based on the decennial census. The surveys of 1976 through 1987 are analyzed in Chapter 8, while this and the following chapters focus on 1985. This year was chosen because it is among the years with the largest sample sizes and it was the last year of 'normal' growth before the succession of both heterodox and orthodox stabilization plans which began in 1986.[7] The survey for 1985 included 479,194 individuals of whom 45,257 (9.4%) were included in the sample studied here. This sample of nonagricultural employees in Brazil's nine major metropolitan regions[8] represents almost one-third of the working-age males surveyed, and almost 40% of those who received remuneration (see Table 4.2). Some general characteristics of the sample are shown in Table 4.3. The composition of the labour force for particular categories is presented in Table 4.4 for comparison.[9]

The choice of sample deserves some attention because it involves a compromise between two different problems related to sample selection and self-selection in the labour market. The first problem arises from excluding population subgroups that should be included; and the second arises from including groups that should be excluded.

The process of selecting the sample should be as inclusive as possible to avoid bias in the estimates. For example, excluding public sector workers would cause an underestimation of the wage advantage for Rio de Janeiro since that sector could provide a significant amount of high wage employment in that city relative to other cities. If the criterion for sample selection is a choice variable, then the conclusions based on a particular subgroup will be particularly questionable. On the other hand, if the selection criterion is not a choice variable, e.g., gender, then the problem may be less serious.

53

Table 4.2
Selection and representativity of sample, PNAD 1985

	Number	Share of Total	Share of Remunerated
Total Persons	479,194	100.0%	
Female	244,783	51.1%	
Male	234,411	48.9%	
Less than 14 Years of Age	83,640	17.5%	
14 Years and Older	150,771	31.5%	
Unremunerated	36,837	7.7%	
Remunerated	113,934	23.8%	100.0%
Not Employee or Self-Employed	12,471	2.6%	10.9%
Employee or Self-Employed	101,463	21.2%	89.1%
Primary Sector	19,130	4.0%	16.8%
Included Sectors	82,333	17.2%	72.3%
Metropolitan Region			
NonResident	36,241	7.6%	31.8%
Resident	46,092	9.6%	40.5%
Missing Data	835	0.2%	0.7%
Final Sample	45,257	9.4%	39.7%

Table 4.3
Sample characteristics for males in the labour force, 1985

Mean Monthly Income   142,390
Calculated Mean Wage   3,069
Mean Log Wage   8.47

Category	Number	Share	Category	Number	Share
Belém	3,570	7.9%	Employee	36,703	81.1%
Fortaleza	3,338	7.4%			
Recife	4,324	9.6%	Occupation:		
Salvador	3,831	8.5%	Miscellaneous	1,539	3.4%
Belo Horizonte	5,796	12.8%	Administrator	3,621	8.0%
Rio de Janeiro	7,028	15.5%	Professional	1,675	3.7%
São Paulo	8,273	18.3%	Technical	2,715	6.0%
Curitiba	3,468	7.7%	Clerical	4,616	10.2%
Porto Alegre	5,629	12.4%	Low Skill Production	12,672	28.0%
			High Skill Production	4,752	10.5%
			Transport & Commun.	3,168	7.0%
			Sales	5,883	13.0%
			Personal Services	4,616	10.2%
Schooling:			Sector:		
0 Years	3,666	8.1%	Heavy Industry	9,549	21.1%
1-4 Years	14,663	32.4%	Light Industry	3,937	8.7%
5-8 Years	14,120	31.2%	Construction	5,702	12.6%
9-11 Years	8,010	17.7%	Commerce	6,789	15.0%
12 or More	4,797	10.6%	Finance	1,946	4.3%
			Transp. and Commun.	3,666	8.1%
			Services	1,946	22.2%
			Public Admin.	3,666	8.0%
Age:					
15-24 Years	12,355	27.3%			
25-34 Years	14,573	32.2%			
35-44 Years	9,459	20.9%			
45-54 Years	5,657	12.5%			
55-64 Years	2,580	5.7%			
65 and Older	634				
Head of Household	31,635	69.9%			

Table 4.4
Composition of regional labour force by sex and employment status, 1985 (%)

Metropolitan Region	Female	Male	Share of males who are:		
			Private Employees	Self-Employed	Public Employees
Belém	29.0	71.0	64.3	12.0	23.7
Fortaleza	38.1	61.9	69.0	9.9	21.1
Recife	31.7	68.3	69.4	9.7	20.9
Salvador	34.0	66.0	71.1	11.4	17.5
Belo Horizonte	31.9	68.1	75.9	7.1	17.0
Rio de Janeiro	29.8	70.2	73.2	11.2	15.6
São Paulo	30.2	69.8	80.6	4.4	15.1
Curitiba	29.9	70.1	71.9	8.8	19.3
Porto Alegre	33.9	66.1	73.4	9.1	17.5
All	31.0	69.0	75.7	7.8	16.5

Source: Author's tabulations from PNAD 1985 data.

Including all workers, however, can also lead to problems. If two population subgroups are confronted by entirely different processes of wage determination, then regressions controlling for the wage determining characteristics will be ineffective. For example, if one group only receives returns to education while the other only receives returns to experience, then the coefficients on these variables will be inaccurately estimated. In this case, the coefficients on the regional dummies will reflect not only level differences between regions, but also the divergence between the 'true' coefficients for each subgroup weighted by their different shares within each region.

Therefore, it is entirely possible for the regional wage differentials ($\varpi_k - \varpi_j$) to be zero for independent subgroups (A and B) conditional on their characteristics (**PC, JC**):

$$E(\varpi_k - \varpi_j \mid \textbf{PC, JC})_A = 0 \qquad\qquad (4.14)$$

$$E(\varpi_k - \varpi_j \mid \textbf{PC, JC})_B = 0, \qquad\qquad (4.15)$$

even though the unconditional and combined expectations are not zero, i.e.,

$$E(\varpi_k - \varpi_j)_{A+B} \neq 0 \text{ and} \qquad\qquad (4.16)$$

$$E(\varpi_k - \varpi_j \mid \textbf{PC, JC })_{A+B} \neq 0. \qquad\qquad (4.17)$$

In fact, this will always be the case whenever the joint distribution of wages (ϖ) and observed factors (**PC, JC**) differ systematically across the two groups and the groups have different regional distributions. In such cases, the expectation in (4.17) which corresponds to the estimates in regression (4.9) would mistakenly indicate regional wage differentials. In fact, separately estimating each distinct subgroup would be preferable and would lead to the results in (4.14) and (4.15).

The problems raised here, whether from inclusion or exclusion of subgroups, become particularly serious when mobility from one subgroup to another is feasible and is subject to choice. Individual's choices, after all, are also affected by the dependent variable. That is, individuals choose to enter particular subgroups — self-employed, urban areas, etc. — depending at least in part on the relative incomes they can obtain. Consequently, dividing the sample between men and women is not likely to create large problems for the hypothesis tests. Excluding public sector or self-employed individuals, however, could generate significant problems. The rest of this section considers the seriousness of these problems for various decisions made in defining the sample.

The sample considered here includes nonagricultural male employees and self-employed workers with positive income residing in Brazil's nine major metropolitan regions. The sample was restricted first of all to urban workers in the metropolitan regions for three reasons. First, it is extremely difficult to compare wage data between urban and rural areas because of nonmonetary payments in rural areas which systematically underestimate earnings. Secondly, cost-of-living comparisons are difficult across metropolitan regions, but would present even greater problems in comparing across urban and rural areas. Finally, since this study tests the proposition that wage differentials may persist across regions in spite of integration, taking the urban areas which are more clearly linked in a national economy makes it possible to test the proposition where it theoretically should hold most strongly. In terms of the problems outlined above, the exclusion of rural workers could lead to overestimates of expected wages in regions where rural workers earn significantly less than their counterparts in other regions, or where they are a larger portion of the labour force.

Table 3.8 showed how the urban composition of the labour force varies considerably across regions. The states of Rio de Janeiro and São Paulo are particularly dominated by their respective metropolitan areas. Figures on the rural population for Pará are not even available in the PNAD survey, but the neighboring state of Maranhão reveals how some areas continue to have a majority of rural residents.

The characteristics of the nonmetropolitan region labour force is also quite different from one region to another. In the state of Pernambuco, proletarianized sugarcane workers predominate in the rural sector, while family farms provide a larger share of employment in Paraná. Productivity also varies dramatically, being generally much lower in the Northeast than in the South and Southeast (see Table 3.8 and Hoffman 1990). Compared to São Paulo, agricultural value added per worker is one-fifth as large in Ceará and one-fourth in Pernambuco. By contrast, the southern states of Paraná and Rio Grande do Sul have rates of productivity which are comparable to São Paulo — ranging from 5% to 20% below that state. The exclusion of the rural sector, then, is clearly a problem for the empirical analysis of regional wage differences. On the other hand, the estimates of regional wage differences generally confirm rather than counter the expected differences between rural earnings. Hence, including the rural sector would produce wider estimates of regional wage differences. Since this study is testing the hypothesis that wages equilibrate across integrated regions, findings of regional wage differences with the rural sector excluded would be stronger evidence for rejecting the hypothesis.

The sample was restricted to men because women's earnings — in addition to being lower than men's on average with lower returns to education and experience (Camargo and Serrano 1983, Birdsall and Behrman 1985) — are strongly affected by factors such as marital status, household status, age, and number of children, in complex ways. Although the share of women in the labour force does not vary dramatically across regions (see Table 4.4) their participation by occupation and sector is quite different, and the regional variation in their educational attainment is quite large. Since men are more geographically mobile than women in Brazil, more likely to follow income opportunities to other areas, the observation of regional wage differentials for men would be a strong indication of regional differences for the labour force as a whole.[10] Although the analysis focused on men, the sensitivity of the conclusions regarding the wage outcomes was tested with a separate estimation of regional wage differentials exclusively for women (see Chapter 6).

A difficult sample choice involved the inclusion of public sector and self-employed individuals. Regions have substantially different compositions of private and public employment and varying opportunities for self-employment.[11] The process by which individuals enter one sector or another is to some degree an outcome of choice. The sample should therefore include all of these subgroups since exclusion could bias the estimates by attributing self-selection or varying composition of employment effects to the regional differential. On the other hand, there is clear evidence that wage determination for these groups differ significantly and that combining all of these groups would bias the estimates of regional differences due to specification error — because of different wage determination processes. Therefore, the groups should be disaggregated for the same reason that women were separated from the sample.

The public sector could be excluded on the grounds that there is relatively little mobility into or out of this sector. However, public sector employment provides alternative careers (and future earnings streams) for individuals entering or only recently entered into the labour force. Furthermore, public sector employment varies significantly as a share of total employment across regions (see Tables 2.2 and 4.4). Since individuals consider a variety of income-earning opportunities, they may very well compare a private sector job in one region and a public sector job in another. That is, people following higher wages in the early part of their careers might compare public employment in Recife with private employment in Belo Horizonte — even though (or precisely because) the outcomes of this decision differ in terms of career ladders, wage determination, and tenure (Macedo 1986). The public sector is included in this study because over long periods of time expected income-earning opportunities should not be able to remain higher in that sector without barriers or rationing of jobs, regardless of the methods of wage determination. As shown below, this decision leads to lower estimates of regional wage dispersion since public sector workers as a group show less regional wage variance when analyzed separately.

Self-employment is frequently associated with 'informal' economic activities in developing countries. Individuals earning income through self-employment could represent hidden unemployment, a residual category of individuals that would be unemployed in a wealthier economy but who seek sustenance in this sector while awaiting opportunities as formal sector employees. On the other hand, the self-employed could represent a sector which is complementary to the formal sector, providing services and goods which are demanded by the formal sector (Marques and Mezerra 1987, Camargo 1989). In the first case, the earnings of the self-employed would be lower wherever formal sector wages are high — driven down by larger numbers of people queuing for formal sector jobs. In the latter case, the earnings of the self-employed would be higher wherever formal sector wages are higher. In Brazil, self-employment appears to be complementary to formal sector employment since there is little mobility from self-employment to formal sector employment.[12] The results of this study will also show that the self-employed tend to earn more in the areas where private sector employees earn more.

The self-employed were included because their earnings are also a potential source for many individuals in the labour market, although their reported earnings may reflect returns which should be attributed to capital. This is especially true because a large proportion of the self-employed are involved in activities with very low levels of capitalization (Duarte 1984, Cavalcanti 1981, Gomes et al 1985, Cacciamali 1983). Since the goal of this study is to detect gaps between income opportunities, being self-employed must also be included as an option which varies systematically across regions (see Table 4.4). The inclusion of the self-employed increases the estimate of regional wage dispersion since, as will be shown below, this subgroup displays larger regional wage variation than the other subgroups.

Finally, it should be noted that the IBGE's methodology involves different sample sizes across the metropolitan regions — from 1/400 in São Paulo to 1/50 in Belém. Consequently, personal weights provided by the IBGE and calculated from the decennial census were used to correct for this. Furthermore, sectoral and occupational disaggregations were reclassified in order to make the surveys from the 1970s comparable to the 1980s. Highly disaggregated data were used to develop consistent categories for an entire decade, from 1976 to 1987. The IBGE's occupational categories closely mimic the sectoral categories at the one-digit level for historical reasons regarding social definitions of 'occupation' in Brazil.[13] For this study, occupational categories were reclassified to group jobs with similar tasks and complexity, more closely in line with international classification schemes.[14]

Notes

1. Only when the quality of workers introduced through migration differs significantly from natives and affects the market significantly will this not hold.

2. Note that I say "expected" because couples where both husband and wife are earning generally report the man as head of household regardless of whether his earnings are the household's main support.

3. Barros and Mendonça (1993) show regional differences have a surprisingly strong impact on earnings indirectly through their effect on educational outcomes.

4. The word "meaningful" is used here to indicate a structural relationship between job characteristics and observed wages.

5. The presence of segmentation between formal and informal sectors, industries, and occupations leading to divergent wages is not restricted to Brazil, and is observed in most modern market and mixed economies — a consequence of supervision costs, efficiency wages, lumpy technology, organizational forms, and selection problems under imperfect information [Doeringer and Piore 1971, Stiglitz 1987, Lang and Leonard (eds.) 1987].

6. See Lehman and Verhina (1986) and Morley (1979); also confirmed in author's interviews in Rio de Janeiro and Recife.

7. IBGE reduced the size of the PNAD sample beginning in 1986 by approximately one-half due to budget cuts. The reliability of the sample was actually improved in some ways because the smaller sample allowed IBGE to train their interviewers and supervise them better. The standard error of the estimates of regional coefficients was not markedly affected by the change in sample size.

8. See Chapter 2 for discussion of metropolitan regions and their definitions.

9. Complete profiles of the labour force and sample are presented in Appendix D of Savedoff (1992).

10. Migration flows are disproportionately male in the working age population. For example, the IBGE's 1977 household survey shows that 72.2% of the individuals living in the metropolitan regions in 1977 who had arrived in the last year were male. Men accounted for 69.6% of all individuals residing in the nine metropolitan regions in 1977 who originated outside their area (author's tabulations from IBGE PNAD data).

11. Opportunities for self-employment may vary significantly across regions due to capital market imperfections. For example, entering retail trade in Fortaleza and Recife is much easier than in São Paulo or Rio de Janeiro because it requires much less capital. São Paulo does have open air markets like the Northeast, but they must compete with highly capitalized supermarkets and department stores. By contrast, the competition in Fortaleza and Recife from such forms of retail trade is more limited. Other economic activities which may be region-specific are more or less technically suited to being organized as a "one person firm". For example, vendors on the beaches of Rio, Recife, and Fortaleza are frequently self-employed. Belo Horizonte, São Paulo, and Curitiba have no beaches to generate such self-employment opportunities.

12. Recent evidence from constructed panel data sets have shown very little mobility between the self-employed and formal sector employees over one to two year periods (Camargo et al, 1990). Mobility over longer periods, however, has not been ruled out by empirical studies.

13. For a discussion of social definitions of work and occupation in Brazil as it affects classifications in census data, see Merrick and Graham (1979), especially Chapter 7 and its appendix.

14. IBGE Classification and Codes were used for sectors of economic activity as follows:

RAM0	Agric/Extr.	Sectors 0-99
		All agriculture and extractive sectors
RAM1	Heavy Ind.	Sectors 100-139, 170-179, 200-209, 230, and 290
		All metallurgy, vehicles, chemicals, ...
RAM2	Light Ind.	Sectors 150-169, 190, 220, and 230-289
		Wood, Furniture, Clothing, Bottling, ...
RAM3	Constr.	Sector 340 - Construction
RAM4	Commerce	Sectors 410-449 and 463
		All commercial activities (retail, wholesale, ...)
RAM5	Finance	Sectors 450-454, 462, and 466
		Banking, Insurance, Real Estate, ...
RAM6	Transport	Sectors 470-482
		Passenger, Cargo, and Communications (postal, telephone, etc..)
RAM7	Services	Sectors 510-600, 461, 610, 612, 613, 615-619, 622-624, and 632
		Tourism, Personal Hygiene, Catering, ...
RAM8	Public Admin.	Sectors 700-730
		Direct public administration
RAM9	Misc.	Sectors 800-999

Occupational categories were constructed as shown below, using a combination of classifications by the IBGE, Medeiros (1982), and Lanzana (1987). The objective was to group those occupations which were most similar in terms of complexity and content of tasks along with degree of decision-making autonomy.

OCC0	Misc.	Miscellaneous
OCC1	Administ	Administrative, management positions
OCC2	Prof	Professionals, Academics, Scientists
OCC3	Tech	Technical personnel, medical technicians, photographers, teachers
OCC4	Clerical	Office personnel
OCC5	Low Skill	Apprentices, unskilled and semi-skilled production positions
OCC6	High Skill	Supervisory or highly skilled production positions
OCC7	Transport	Positions in transportation (drivers, pilots) and communications (postal carriers, operators)
OCC8	Sales	All sales positions
OCC9	Pers./Serv.	Personal and other services (barbers, elevator operators, waiters, ...)

A detailed listing of the groupings of occupational and sectoral categories at the three digit level can be found in Appendix C of Savedoff (1992). The composition of the regional labor force by these categories can be found in Appendix D of Savedoff (1992).

5 Estimating regional wage differences: Controlling for composition effects

This chapter will investigate regional wage differentials with a cross-sectional and static analysis of household survey data from 1985 in order to evaluate the compositional factors which affect regional comparisons. It will show that the composition of the work force and the regional composition of jobs can explain only part of the variation in earnings across regions. It will conclude that regional variation in wages is significant, although it is overshadowed by personal and job characteristics in explaining total wage variation.

Findings: nominal regional wage differences in Brazil

The regional differences in median wages presented in Table 2.1 are only a simple description of the regional wage differences. The various specifications presented in Chapter 4 make it possible to consider whether these regional differences are solely the result of differing regional composition of the labour force and jobs, or whether they remain robust after controls for these factors are introduced.

For this analysis, four earnings equations were estimated, each of which included dummy variables for metropolitan region of residence. The first equation (5.1) regresses log wages on the regional dummy variables alone, in order to calculate the average uncontrolled differences between regions. The second equation (5.2) regresses log wages on a linear combination of the regional dummy variables and a set of personal characteristics, including age, education, and head of household status.   The third equation (5.3) regresses log wages on the regional dummy variables and a set of variables representing job characteristics. Finally, equation (5.4) regresses log wages on the regional dummy variables and all of the other variables, personal and job characteristics combined. The coefficients on the regional dummy variables in the latter three earnings equations are controlled for the impact of the other variables and represent the 'true' regional wage differences under the various definitions and the particular assumptions regarding left-out variables and orthogonality discussed in Chapter 4.

$$\varpi_i = \alpha_1 + \mathbf{R}_i\, \rho_1 + \qquad\qquad \epsilon_{1i} \qquad\qquad (5.1)$$

$$\varpi_i = \alpha_2 + \mathbf{R}_i\, \rho_2 + \mathbf{PC}_i\, \varphi_2 + \qquad \epsilon_{2i} \qquad\qquad (5.2)$$

$$\varpi_i = \alpha_3 + \mathbf{R}_i\, \rho_3 + \qquad + \mathbf{JC}_i\, \gamma_3 + \epsilon_{3i} \qquad\qquad (5.3)$$

$$\varpi_i = \alpha_4 + \mathbf{R}_i\, \rho_4 + \mathbf{PC}_i\, \varphi_4 + \mathbf{JC}_i\, \gamma_4 + \epsilon_{4i} \qquad\qquad (5.4)$$

where:

ϖ = log hourly wage;

α = constant term;

$\mathbf{R}$ = an 8-column matrix of dummy variables for metropolitan region;

$\mathbf{PC}$ = a vector of variables representing personal characteristics: 4 dummy variables for educational categories, 5 for age categories, and 1 for head of household status;

$\mathbf{JC}$ = a vector of variables representing the individual's job characteristics: 9 dummies for occupational categories, 8 for sector of activity, and 1 to distinguish employees from the self-employed;

φ, γ, and ρ = vectors of associated coefficients; and

ϵ = error term, assumed to be orthogonal to included variables.

The results of regressions (5.1) through (5.4) are reported in Table 5.1. The coefficients on age, education, head of household status, occupation, and sector are all statistically significant, and the R^2 of the equations with control variables ranges from 33.3% to 55.3%. The coefficients on the regional dummy variables show, for example, that under the assumption that place of residence is uncorrelated with personal and job characteristics [equation (5.1)] an individual can expect to earn 53.2% less on average in Fortaleza than in São Paulo — which was the excluded region. Since regression (5.1) is the unconditional expectation of log wages, it closely reflects the ranking and relative wage differences of the median wages presented in Table 2.1.[1]

The coefficients on the regional dummy variables represent the percentage difference between wages in a particular region compared to São Paulo.[2]

For ease of interpretation, a linear transformation was applied to the regional dummy variable coefficients — a simple 'shift' of the base or comparison from São Paulo to the overall sample mean.[3] The results are reported in Table 5.2. With this transformation, it becomes possible to discuss each

Table 5.1
Estimated coefficients for earnings functions, 1985

Regressions	(5.1)	(5.2)	(5.3)	(5.4)
Sample	45,257	45,257	45,257	45,257
Model d.f.	8	18	25	35
Sum of Squares	247,106	4,391,884	2,888,885	4,806,431
F-Value	165	2,570	902	1,601
R-Squared	0.028	0.506	0.333	0.553
Intercept	8.69	7.31	9.58	7.88
Belém	-0.248	-0.336	-0.195	0.271
Fortaleza	-0.532	-0.456	-0.431	-0.408
Recife	-0.524	-0.462	-0.429	-0.417
Salvador	-0.229	-0.268	-0.199	-0.230
Belo Horizonte	-0.273	-0.257	-0.249	-0.238
Rio de Janeiro	-0.245	-0.369	-0.223	-0.318
São Paulo	*	*	*	*
Curitiba	-0.118	-0.205	-0.126	-0.179
Porto Alegre	-0.074	-0.187	-0.081	-0.163
Schooling: 0 Years		*		*
1-4 Years		8.385		0.311
5-7 Years		0.716		0.579
8-11 Years		1.290		1.033
12 or More		0.090		1.645
Age: 15-24 Years		*		*
25-34 Years		0.359		0.323
35-44 Years		0.557		0.503
45-54 Years		0.581		0.528
55-64 Years		0.466		0.440
65 and older		0.337		0.312
Head of Household		0.403		0.374
Employee		-0.064		0.007#

(Table 5.1 continued on next page)

Table 5.1 (continued)

Regressions	(5.1)	(5.2)	(5.3)	(5.4)
Occupation:				
Miscellaneous			-0.695	-0.326
Administrator			*	*
Professional			0.913	0.279
Technical			-0.218	-0.082
Clerical			-0.497	-0.234
Low Skill Prod.			-1.002	-0.370
High Skill Prod.			-0.588	-0.116
Transp. & Commun.			-0.520	-0.150
Sales			-0.611	-0.223
Personal Services			-1.150	-0.531
Sector:				
Heavy Industry			*	*
Light Industry			-0.295	-0.179
Construction			-0.497	-0.293
Commerce			-0.515	-0.316
Finance			0.337	0.249
Transp. & Commun.			-0.20	-0.064
Services			-0.47	-0.246
Public Admin.			-0.011#	-0.059

Notes: Total Sum of Squares 8,686,022   Mean Log Wage = 8.53   #indicates not significant at the 0.1% level

region relative to the sample mean, rather than in comparison only with São Paulo. For example, Table 5.2 shows that, conditional on personal and job characteristics [equation (5.1)], individuals in Fortaleza earn about 37.5% below the mean wage for all workers in the sample; while individuals in São Paulo earn 15.6% above the overall mean.[4]

Table 5.2
Estimates of regional wage differentials, 1985

Metropolitan Region	Differences from Sample Mean				
	Eq. 5.1	Eq. 5.2	Eq. 5.3	Eq. 5.4	N
Belém	-9.2%	-14.1%	-5.7%	-10.0%	3,570
Fortaleza	-37.5%	-26.2%	-29.3%	-23.7%	3,338
Recife	-36.8%	-26.7%	-29.1%	-24.6%	4,324
Salvador	-7.3%	-7.3%	-6.1%	-5.9%	3,831
Belo Horizonte	-11.7%	-6.2%	-11.1%	-6.7%	5,796
Rio de Janeiro	-8.9%	-17.3%	-8.5%	-14.7%	7,028
São Paulo	15.6%	19.5%	13.8%	17.1%	8,273
Curitiba	3.8%	-0.7%	1.2%	-0.8%	3,468
Porto Alegre	8.2%	0.9%	5.7%	0.8%	5,629
Standard Deviation (Adj. & Wtd.)	14.4%	16.2%	12.1%	14.1%	

Notes: All coefficients are significant at the 1% level.

The ranking of uncontrolled nominal wage differentials is not unexpected in some ways, but quite surprising in others (see Table 5.2). Fortaleza and Recife are well below the sample average (about 37% below) as might be expected given their low levels of education, low productivity industries and technologies, and high portion of informal economic activities. São Paulo is well above the national average (15.6%) as might be expected given its dynamic, highly productive, industrialized economy. Curitiba and Porto Alegre are also above the national average, but surprisingly the expected wage in Salvador is higher than in Rio de Janeiro and Belo

Horizonte. These latter two cities have long histories as centres for production and commerce in Brazil, yet their wage levels seem to place them below Salvador which experienced slow growth after the decline of the sugar economy in the 18th century and has begun to expand rapidly again only in the last twenty years. Belém is below the national average, but is a special case given its relative isolation from the rest of the country.

Dramatic differences exist between cities which are somewhat close: 24% between Rio and São Paulo, and 29% between Recife and Salvador. The standard errors for these estimates are reasonably small [.018 on average for regression (5.1)], with all of the measured differences statistically significant at the 0.1% level. The magnitudes of the wage differences can be summarized by the weighted and adjusted standard deviation of 17.0%.[5]

Introducing controls: personal characteristics

The dramatic findings of Table 5.2 are to be found when comparing these average uncontrolled differences with the controlled differences. The basic pattern of regional nominal wage differentials, which has been attributed to different regional compositions of the work force and jobs, is highly invariant to the addition of controls for these factors except in a few cases. Although it increases the explanatory power of the regression by some 47% (see Table 5.1), the addition of information about individuals' education, age, and household status, does not alter the ranking of wage differences very much nor eliminate the regional variations as is apparent from the high correlation between the two sets of estimates (see Table 5.3).

Table 5.3
Correlations of various estimations of regional wage differentials

	No Controls (1)	Personal Controls (2)	Job Controls (3)	All Controls (4)
No Controls	1.000			
Personal Controls	0.929	1.000		
Job Controls	0.996	0.949	1.000	
All Controls	0.939	0.999	0.958	1.000

Note: All correlations significant at the 1% level. Correlations are sample weighted.

Adjusting for the regional differences in composition of the work force by education, age, and household status significantly changes only the ranking of two cities — Belo Horizonte which has a significantly higher expected wage level and Rio de Janeiro which has a significantly lower level. Salvador's rank changes only because of the effect of the changes for these other two cities since its expected wage level is the same with or without the inclusion of personal characteristics. The other six cities — São Paulo, Curitiba, Porto Alegre, Belém, Recife, and Fortaleza[6] — retain their relative positions. The stability of the nominal wage rankings for seven of the nine cities indicates that these regional wage differentials are not purely a phenomenon of work force composition, or any factor which is highly correlated with work force composition.

The estimated magnitudes of regional wage differences change in significant ways with the inclusion of controls for personal characteristics. The work force composition of Fortaleza and Recife — with lower than average education and age — account for a large part of the wage disadvantage in these cities. This explains why equation (5.1) yields a larger wage gap from the mean (37%) for these cities than equation (5.2) which adjusts for work force composition (26%). Belém has a lower expected wage level, farther from the sample mean, when adjustment is made for its relatively high educational standing. Rio de Janeiro's expected wage conditional on education falls much farther below the sample mean than the average wage without controls for much the same reason. Rio's average educational level is significantly higher than in the other metropolitan regions without an accompanying advantage in wages; hence the level comparison shows that a worker with comparable education and age earns on average 17% less than the national mean in Rio de Janeiro while the unconditional mean wage difference is only 9%.

Belo Horizonte, Curitiba, and Porto Alegre all move toward the mean in this specification. In the case of Curitiba and Porto Alegre, their higher than average wage levels are closely associated with their higher than average educational levels. In Belo Horizonte, the city's wage disadvantage of almost 12% in the uncontrolled estimation (5.1) appears to be somewhat overstated by the lower than average educational attainment of its work force, so the resulting estimated wage gap is only half as much (6%).

Interestingly, the expected wage conditional on personal characteristics in São Paulo is even farther above the mean than in the uncontrolled regression. Although São Paulo has wages much above the mean, the average educational attainment is much closer to the average of the nine urban areas (see Table 2.2). São Paulo's wage advantage cannot, then, be explained by observed work force characteristics.

In three cities — Belém, Rio, and São Paulo — the effect of introducing personal characteristics moves the estimated wage level away from the sample mean. The expected wage level conditional on personal characteristics in Rio and Belém is farther below the mean than the unconditional expectation, while the conditional mean is farther above the mean in São Paulo. The contrast between Rio and São Paulo could indicate differences in urban amenities. Rio is frequently described as a more desirable city because of a more relaxed life style, less pollution, beaches, and its cultural attributes. There are two problems with such an interpretation, however. First, São Paulo is a very active cultural and social centre in its own right with numerous other amenities. Second, Belém also moves below the mean even though it has few of the advantages claimed by Rio.

The key to understanding these three cases may lie in the interpretation of this conditional mean. Recalling the discussion in chapter 4, the expected wage level conditional on personal characteristics treats job composition and region-wide productivity differences as region-specific, or rather, attributes any influence on wages which is not evenly distributed spatially as a regional factor. Industry is among the highest paid sectors of economic activity, and São Paulo has a third of its labour force employed in this sector. Rio and Belém, by contrast, have half this share of employment in industry.

Quality of education may also affect the variables. Essentially the estimates indicate a higher return in São Paulo for people with comparable years of schooling. It could be that schooling in São Paulo is of better quality in terms of remunerated skills. Although the opposite case could be made for Belém (i.e., that school quality may be lower than average), it is unlikely to hold for Rio de Janeiro which has traditionally had one of the better schooling systems in the country.

Because regions are so complex, all three of these issues may be of importance. Rio may maintain a lower mean conditional on education because of offsetting amenities, while São Paulo could be higher due to its large share of industrial employment and better school quality. Belém's wage level may be lower because of poorer schooling. Only detailed comparison of the regional economies can evaluate these hypotheses.

In sum, adjusting for labour force composition using observed personal characteristics moves the expected wage level in three cities away from the mean, leaves one unchanged (Salvador), and moves the other five toward the mean. The overall effect is a compression of the wage differentials when controlled for personal characteristics. Consequently the overall dispersion declines, but only by some 12%, from 0.170 to 0.149, as measured by the standard deviation of the differentials. This confirms that wages vary systematically across regions independently of observed labour quality. It is the first evidence that market forces may not be operative across regions in Brazil.

Introducing controls: job characteristics

The third column of Table 5.2 shows the estimated regional wage differences after controlling for job characteristics. These are estimated with regression 5.3 and measure whether average wage differences across the cities can be attributed to regional differences in composition by sector of economic activity, occupation, and whether or not the worker was an employee. This regression explains some 30% more of the variation in log earnings than regression (5.1), but once again it has fairly limited impact upon the ranking or dispersion of regional wage differentials, and is highly correlated with the original uncontrolled estimates (see Table 5.3).

Changes in ranking are minor, with Belém and Salvador exchanging positions. Again, the rankings of São Paulo, Porto Alegre, Curitiba, Fortaleza and Recife remain unchanged. Belo Horizonte's expected wage level is unaffected by the inclusion of job characteristics. This time the alteration in rankings occurs among Belém, Rio de Janeiro, and Salvador, but solely because the expected wage conditional on job characteristics in Belém increases substantially and rises above the level in both Salvador and Rio. The job controls do not significantly change the estimated wage differential for Rio or Salvador at all. The adjustment for composition of jobs in each region does not really affect the rankings at all except for the shift of Belém.

Compared to the estimation with personal characteristics, the inclusion of job characteristics has a more uniform impact on the magnitudes of the regional wage differentials. The changes which occur are consistently toward the mean, never away from it. The job controls have a large impact on the estimated wage differentials in Fortaleza, Recife, and Belém. In two cases there are significant but much smaller movements toward the mean — in São Paulo (15.6% to 13.8%) and Porto Alegre (8.2% to 5.7%). Elsewhere, in Salvador, Belo Horizonte, Rio de Janeiro, and Curitiba, the adjustment for job composition does not significantly change the estimated wage differences.

The adjustment for job composition reduces the overall dispersion by almost 20%, from 0.170 to 0.137, as measured by the standard deviation of the differentials. Note that, although the job characteristics by themselves explain less of the overall dispersion of log earnings than the personal characteristics, they account for a larger share of the dispersion in regional wage levels. This results from its more uniform impact on bringing wage

71

differentials closer to the mean in all cases where significant changes occurred and leaving the remainder largely the same with no significant divergence from the mean. This suggests that the regional wage differences are more a consequence of regionally divergent job opportunities than of the different populations residing in each region. In no case were high wage levels associated with a regional concentration of low wage sectors and occupations nor were lower than average wage levels associated with regional concentrations of high wage sectors and occupations. This contrasts with the analysis of personal characteristics where particular cases (Rio de Janeiro, São Paulo, and Belém) revealed an inverse relationship between work force composition and the expected wage level.

Introducing controls: combined characteristics

Personal and job characteristics are so highly correlated, that when combined in the final regression (5.9) the dispersion of regional wage differentials hardly declines at all. The final ranking of regions is largely preserved relative to the ranking without any controls, and the magnitudes of the wage differential remain significantly different from zero. These estimates are also highly correlated with the original uncontrolled estimates (see Table 5.3).

In this specification, the rankings are preserved for all of the cities except Belém, Belo Horizonte, and Rio de Janeiro. The rankings change because of Rio de Janeiro's sharp decline (-9% to -15%) and Belo Horizonte's significant climb (-12% to -7%) relative to the uncontrolled estimates [equation (5.1)]. Belém's rank changes, but its estimated wage level relative to the mean is essentially the same as in the uncontrolled estimate.

The magnitudes of the wage differentials are altered by the inclusion of personal and job characteristics in seven of the nine cities. São Paulo remains the highest wage area, and its expected wage conditional on both job and personal characteristics is 17.1% above the sample mean. If this is the correct specification, then the simple averages [15.6% from equation (5.1)] understate the extent of São Paulo's true regional wage advantage. In two cases, Curitiba and Porto Alegre, the composition effects appear to account for all of the divergence from the sample mean, and this is largely attributable to the inclusion of the personal characteristic variables, as the comparison in Table 5.2 shows. The impact on the expected wage in Fortaleza and Recife of adjusting for both work force and job composition is significant, with the resulting wage gap reduced to about 24%. These two cities, however, remain well below the national average in terms of wage levels even after the adjustments are made. Salvador remains in fourth place after Curitiba, with its expected wage level still below the sample mean and largely unaffected by the inclusion of controls. As mentioned above, Rio de Janeiro's wage level conditional on both job and personal characteristics is quite far below the mean, and significantly lower than in the uncontrolled estimation. In this specification (5.4), Belo Horizonte appears to have a wage level significantly closer to the sample mean than the uncontrolled estimates (5.1) would indicate.

Relative to the first uncontrolled estimation (5.1), the coefficients for the regional variables are statistically indistinguishable between Salvador and Belém. In the cases of Fortaleza, Recife, Belo Horizonte, Curitiba, and Porto Alegre, the controlled estimates are closer to the mean; while the estimates for Rio de Janeiro and São Paulo diverge significantly from the mean. Overall the regional wage pattern — in ranking, magnitudes, and dispersion — is not substantially altered by the inclusion of both sets of controls. This is remarkable given that the inclusion of these factors raises the R^2 from around 3% to over 55%. The personal and job characteristics account for an enormous amount of wage variation, but very little of the regional variation. They do account for some of the regional wage divergence from the mean in five cases, but not in the other four. Furthermore, Rio de Janeiro represents an extreme case in which the unconditional expected wage level bears no significant relationship to the regional composition of either jobs or workers.

This final specification completes the set of estimates. All four specifications produce comparable results in terms of rankings. The inclusion of control variables reduces the dispersion of the regional wage differences, but does not uniformly reduce the gap between regional wage levels and the sample mean.

The contribution of regional wage differentials to total income inequality

The foregoing analysis confirms the existence of regional nominal wage differentials after adjusting for personal and job composition of the different metropolitan areas. Brazil's income distribution is highly concentrated and much debate has focused on the factors which contribute to this skewed distribution. Could the regional wage differentials be a major factor in contributing to income inequality in Brazil?

This section utilizes analysis of covariance to evaluate the importance of regional wage variation in the overall distribution of earnings[7]. An upper bound is estimated using the proportion of wage variance accounted for in a regression which includes only one particular set of variables (e.g., personal characteristics, job characteristics, region) as measured by the R-squared. The lower bound is the proportion of wage variance which the particular set of variables contributes to the model *after all other variables have already been included*. The lower bound, then, measures how much the model's predictive power improves with the addition of a particular variable.[8] The results of this analysis of covariance appear in Table 5.4.

Table 5.4
Analysis of covariance for selected years

	Personal Characteristics	Job Characteristics	Metropolitan Region
PNAD 1985 (N = 45,256) R-Square = 0.55			
Lower Bound	22.4%	4.8%	1.6%
Upper Bound	46.9%	30.9%	2.8%
No. of Variables	10	17	8
# of Covariate Cells	877	487	2836
Ave. Observations per cell	46.70	84.10	14.50
PNAD 1987 (N = 24,867) R-Square = 0.55			
Lower Bound	21.4%	4.4%	4.7%
Upper Bound	53.6%	28.9%	5.3%
No. of Categories	10	17	8
PNAD 1976 (N = 22,515) R-Square = 0.46			
Lower Bound	14.3%	4.8%	3.7%
Upper Bound	37.0%	29.2%	3.4%
No. of Categories	10	17	8

Note: All correlations are significant at the 1% level.

As can be seen for selected years, the proxies for personal productivity contribute significantly to the overall observed variation in wages, from 22% to 47% of the total variation.[9] The job structure accounts for between 4.8% and 30.9% of the variance in log earnings. By contrast, the categories of metropolitan regions explain at most 2.8% of the variation in log earnings.

This small contribution of regional effects to the overall distribution of wages is found in other studies as well. After accounting for urban/rural wage differences in Colombia, Fields and Schultz (1980) found that adding variables for Departments[10] contributed only 'modestly' to the explanatory power of the models, as measured by the increase in the R^2 from 0.339 to 0.367. Fishlow (1972) applied an alternative inequality measure, the Theil index, to decompose Brazilian income inequality using 1970 census data and also found that regional differences are less important than education, age, and sector of economic activity in accounting for total income inequality.

The small contribution to total income dispersion, however, does not mean that regional differences are insignificant. In part, it shows the independence of the regional wage structure in relation to other factors. Were it more highly correlated with the included personal and job characteristics, the range of explanatory power associated with region would be greater without signifying anything more than that it was correlated with other factors. The relative independence of regional effects is apparent in the high correlation between the unadjusted regional wage differentials and the differentials after adjustment for potential covariates, 0.939 (see Table 5.3). Although regional variation does not explain much of the overall dispersion of wages, the part of variation accounted for by the controls does not markedly reduce this regional impact. That is, the regional pattern is highly orthogonal to personal characteristics, occupation, and sector of activity, so its range of contribution is tighter. Personal and job characteristics, by contrast, can both explain substantial portions of wage dispersion, but are so highly correlated as to make separation of their effects extremely difficult.

The regional wage differentials, then, are significant in the sense that expected wages are not equal across regions, even after accounting for almost half the dispersion in wages by use of control variables. These regional wage differences, however, are not as important in explaining the overall dispersion of wages as are personal and job characteristics. Nevertheless, the regional effects are largely independent of the mean effects of other included variables, as shown by the robustness of the regional estimates to the various specifications in the previous sections.

Summary of findings

In five cases, the composition effects account for much of the regional wage gap (Fortaleza, Recife, Belo Horizonte, Curitiba, and Porto Alegre). In Fortaleza and Recife, for example, the adjustments for relatively low educational levels and low wage economic activities show that expected wages conditional on these factors are not as large as might be suggested by the simple unconditional mean. Curitiba and Porto Alegre represent the opposite case, where higher than average unconditional wages are largely accounted for by composition effects. In two cases (Belém and Salvador), however, the regional composition has little bearing upon the observed average wage differences. Furthermore, in two important cases, Rio de Janeiro and São Paulo, the composition effects do not account for the expected wage difference from the mean at all. In São Paulo, the expected wage advantage relative to the mean is actually higher after adjusting for the regional composition of the work force and jobs, whereas in Rio the expected wage disadvantage relative to the mean is even lower when adjustments are made for that city's high educational levels.

The dispersion of the regional wage differentials — as measured by the standard deviation of the regional wage coefficients — is a summary measure of the changing magnitudes of regional differentials. In every specification the inclusion of more variables reduces the standard deviation of the regional wage pattern. The inclusion of personal characteristics reduces the overall dispersion by 12% while the job characteristics introduced in equation (5.3) reduce the overall dispersion by 20%. When combined, job and personal characteristics together account for some 22% of the dispersion of unconditional mean wage differences across regions.

Although interesting changes occur from one specification to the next, the overall pattern of nominal wage differentials — ranking, magnitudes, and dispersion — is robust to the inclusion of other factors. The estimated wage differentials in each of these specifications are highly correlated. Observed regional differences in work force and job composition, then, cannot explain the observed divergence in wages across Brazil's nine major metropolitan regions. Nevertheless, analysis of covariance shows that the observed personal and job characteristics overshadow regional differences in explaining the overall distribution of income despite the statistical significance of the regional wage differences.

Notes

1. The difference between regional median wages will not be exactly the same as the difference between the least mean square average estimated in regression (4.1) except in perfectly symmetric distributions because the two measures of central tendency diverge for asymmetric distributions. Wages are approximately distributed log normally, however, and therefore the log transformation applied to the observed wage maps the dependent variable into a more symmetric distribution.

2. Actually, the coefficient is a log approximation of the actual percentage difference between regions. Throughout this study, the log approximation is used since the correction has no significant impact on the findings. For comparison, see the corrected estimates in Appendix D in Savedoff (1992).

3. In particular, the regression yields the coefficients f_i which estimate by what percentage the average wage in region i differs from the average wage in the excluded metropolitan region (São Paulo). Let f be a vector of 9 coefficients, where $f_k = 0$ for the excluded metropolitan region. Then a simple linear transformation makes it possible to adjust the coefficients to show the deviation of regional wages from the mean, i.e.

$$\phi_i = f_i - (1/N) \sum n_j \cdot f_j$$

where n_j is the number of workers in department j, and

$$N = \sum n_j$$

Let A be a square matrix whose elements in each column j are the share of observations in region j, that is $a_{ij} = n_j/N$. Then the equation can be rewritten in matrix form as:

$$\phi = (I - A) f.$$

The variance of the coefficients, the diagonal elements of the covariance matrix Δ_f, then must be adjusted as

$$\Delta = (I - A) \Delta_f (I - A)'$$

The square roots of the diagonal elements of matrix Δ are then adjusted standard deviations for ϕ, the new coefficient vector. The adjusted vector, showing the regional wage structure for 1985 appears in Table 5.2.

4. The sum of the transformed figures differs from the coefficient in the regression by 0.1% due to rounding.

5. The standard deviations are weighted by the sample size in each city. This corrects the standard deviation from being sensitive to small outliers. The weighting tends to reduce the measured standard deviation in this case because the larger cities, Rio and São Paulo, are closer to the mean than cities like Fortaleza, Recife, or Belém.

   The standard is also adjusted for the estimation error of the coefficients. Since the regional wage differences are themselves measured with error, the standard error of their measurement would tend to overestimate the true dispersion of the coefficients. Therefore, the adjusted standard deviation is a better measure of the average variation between regions. The adjustment estimates the true dispersion, σ, as:

$$\sigma = \hat{\sigma} - 1/K \sum \sigma(\beta_k),$$

where $\hat{\sigma}$ is the standard deviation of the regional dummy coefficients (β_k), and $\sigma(\beta_k)$ is the standard error of β_k.

6. Strictly speaking, Fortaleza and Recife exchange positions, but the estimated differences between these two cities are statistically insignificant in all four specifications. It is more accurate to describe them as "tied" in last place in each estimation.

7. The inequality measure utilized here is the variance. This measure has the advantage of being decomposable by standard regression methods and has direct interpretation from standard analysis of covariance techniques. Variance is not the only decomposable inequality measure, and other indices such as the Theil index are sometimes preferable (see Bourgignon 1979 and Shorrocks 1980). The variance was chosen for simplicity since it followed directly from the models presented above. Fishlow (1972) conducted a decomposition of Brazilian income distribution utilizing a Theil index and 1970 preliminary census data. His conclusions regarding the relatively small importance of region in the overall distribution of income are confirmed for the earnings distribution in 1985 in the following analysis.

8. See Hendry and Marshall (1983) for some problems with interpreting lower and upper bound measures. The alternative of simulating inequality by substituting alternative distributions of explanatory variables was unnecessary and would yield similar conclusions.

9. It is important to remember that interpreting human capital proxies is problematic since it is difficult to distinguish social selection mechanisms from returns to embodied productivity.

10. These are political subdivisions in Colombia which are roughly comparable to states in the U.S. or provinces in Canada.

6 Regional wage differentials for labour force subgroups

The previous chapter essentially tested a null model involving a nationally homogeneous labour market for males with positive earnings residing in the nine major metropolitan regions. The joint hypothesis that all regional coefficients are zero was rejected at a high confidence level. The rejection held for a variety of specifications, and is, therefore, robust across the range of models which were estimated. Nevertheless, the null model implicitly assumes general equilibrium in the labour market with few constraints to economic behaviour. Rejecting the hypothesis, then, can also be the result of problems with these two assumptions, i.e., that (1) the market is not in equilibrium, or (2) the sample includes subgroups with distinct wage determination processes, systematically different regional distributions, and obstacles to mobility across these categories. This chapter will address the second possibility, that of misspecification due to combining heterogenous wage determination categories or excluding relevant groups. The possibility of disequilibrium will be addressed later within a dynamic framework (see Chapters 8 and 9).

Private employees, public employees, and the self-employed

The sample is already relatively homogeneous since it includes only males in nonagricultural activities with positive earnings who reside in the major urban areas. As discussed in Chapter 4, the major differences within the sample in terms of wage determination have to do with combining the categories of private, public, and self-employment. To evaluate the sensitivity of the statistical test and estimates to the combination of self-employed, public sector, and private sector employees, separate estimates were made for each of these groups. Except where noted, the regional wage differences that are reported were estimated with regression (5.4), that is, with controls for both personal and job characteristics. The high correlation of these differentials across the four specifications made it unnecessary to report all of the alternative estimates. In all cases, the estimated dispersion of regional wages was lowest for the reported specification, and represents in some sense a lower bound for regional wage variation.

In each of these cases, the null hypothesis of no regional wage differentials was easily rejected at the 0.1% confidence level. The ranking of the regional wage differentials was broadly comparable across these groups in the following sense. In all cases, São Paulo was the highest wage city. Also, Curitiba and Porto Alegre consistently followed in either second or third place. Fortaleza and Recife were consistently among the three lowest-wage cities.

Largely due to the similar regional rankings across private employees, public employees and the self-employed, the regional wage differentials estimated for each group separately were highly correlated with one another. Table 6.1 shows the estimates for regional wage differentials for each subgroup [using equation (5.4)] and Table 6.2 shows the unweighted correlations between these estimates. In most cases, the correlation is significant at the 1% level. These correlations show that the private sector regional wage differentials are broadly similar to those of the public sector (0.888) and also correlated with the self-employed (0.747). By contrast, the relationship between regional wage patterns of the public sector and the self-employed is much weaker (0.589). Aside from this broad comparability, however, the estimated regional wage gaps differ importantly from one group to the next.

Table 6.1
Controlled nominal wage differentials across regions by employment status, 1985

Metropolitan Region	Differences from Sample Mean (%)				
	Private Employees (1)	All Employees (2)	Self-Employed (3)	Public Employees (4)	Entire Sample (5)
Belém	-13.4	-13.2	1.2	-7.7	-10.0
Fortaleza	-27.6	-27.2	-12.6	-24.0	-23.7
Recife	-16.8	-16.0	-42.0	-10.8	-24.6
Salvador	-3.0	-3.2	-8.6	-3.9	-5.9
Belo Horizonte	-6.4	-6.0	-7.8	-4.7	-6.7
Rio de Janeiro	-14.7	-13.4	-17.8	0.6	-14.7
São Paulo	14.7	14.8	23.7	8.1	17.1
Curitiba	4.0	-3.4	7.9	3.3	-0.8
Porto Alegre	0.7	0.7	4.1	4.8	0.8
Standard Deviations (%)					
All Controls	11.0	10.7	15.5	4.5	12.0
w/No Controls	16.6	15.1	28.1	10.4	17.0
w/Personal Control	15.6	14.7	20.4	8.2	14.9
w/Job Controls	11.1	11.0	22.5	10.8	13.7
Correlations of Controlled and Uncontrolled Coefficients					
Correlation	0.94	0.92	0.97	0.97	0.93

Notes: 1. Controlled Nominal Wage Differentials are expected percentage difference from sample mean wage conditional on all personal and job characteristic variables[i.e., linearly transformed coefficients from regression (5.4)].
2. Correlations reported between regional dummy coefficients with no other variables included [regression (5.1)] and coefficients from regression (5.4), and all are significant at the 1% level.
3. Standard deviations are adjusted for estimation error and weighted by the sample size in each metropolitan region.

Table 6.2
Correlation between subsample wage differentials

	Private Employees (1)	All Employees (2)	Self- Employed (3)	Public Employees (4)	Entire Sample (5)
Private Employees	1.000	0.979	0.747	0.888	0.954
All Employees		1.000	0.715	0.883	0.956
Self-Employed			1.000	0.589	0.888
Public Employees				1.000	0.831
Entire Sample					1.000
t-Statistics for Correlations (with 7 Degrees of Freedom)					
Private Employees	-	12.77 ***	2.97 **	5.10 ***	8.42 ***
All Employees	-	-	2.71**	4.97 ***	8.58 ***
Self-Employed	-	-	-	1.93 *	5.11 ***
Public Employees	-	-	-	-	3.95 ***
Entire Sample	-	-	-	-	-

Note: These correlations are unweighted and unadjusted. As described in the text, weighted and adjusted correlations would be even higher. *** = significant at 1% level; ** = 5% level; and * = 10%.

Although São Paulo is the highest wage city in all three cases, its wage advantage is extremely high among self-employed workers (23.7%), high among private employees (14.7%), and moderate among public sector workers (8.1%). In Curitiba, the self-employed enjoy a 7.9% wage advantage, while the premium for public and private employees is only one-half of that (3.3% and 4.0%, respectively). Porto Alegre's private employees earn close to the sample mean, while the self-employed and public sector employees earn some 4% above the mean. Salvador and Belo Horizonte have expected wage levels below the mean in all three cases, ranging from -3% to -8.6%. In both of these cities, the self-employed earn significantly less (relative to their peers in other cities) than private or public employees. Rio has a strong wage disadvantage for both private employees and the self-employed, but its public sector workers earn at the sample mean. The self-employed fare relatively better in Belém, and much worse in Recife (-42%). In Fortaleza, self-employed workers do well (−12%) relative to employees in the private and public sectors (-27% and −24%, respectively).

The estimated wage differentials for the privately and publicly employed are quite similar. If Rio is excluded, the ranking of the cities for these two groups is the same. Furthermore, the magnitudes of the regional wage differences are generally smaller for the public sector but still bear some resemblance to the private sector differentials. In three cases (Curitiba, Belo Horizonte, and Salvador) the difference between the estimates is not even statistically significant .

By contrast, the wage differentials for the self-employed are much more dispersed and bear less of a relationship to the estimates for the entire sample. A substantial part of the variation discussed above actually results from the regional wage pattern of the self-employed and not from differences between the private and public employees. In Belém, Fortaleza, Recife, São Paulo, and Curitiba, the self-employed do considerably better than the private or publicly employed in the same regions. In Recife, the self-employed do considerably worse (-42%) compared to the entire sample (-24.6%).

As the largest part of the total sample, private employees have a strong impact on the regional differences reported in Chapter 5. They also represent an intermediate case, in terms of regional wage dispersion, between the public sector and the self-employed. Table 6.1 shows that the regional dispersion of wages for private employees is close to the dispersion estimated for the entire sample (12% and 12.2%, respectively). By contrast, the regional dispersion of expected wages is much larger for the self-employed (17.4%) and much smaller for the public sector (9.2%).

The dispersion is a summary measure of the magnitudes of the regional wage differentials, which are generally largest for the self-employed, smaller for the private sector employees, and smallest for public sector employees.

The higher dispersion for the self-employed indicates that regional differences in employer-employee relationships are probably not a central factor in explaining regional nominal wage differences. Instead, there are other factors affecting self-employment earnings which may also affect the relative earnings of employees.

At this point it is worth noting which factors cannot explain the pattern of regional wage differences exhibited by the self-employed. First, the number of self-employed as a share of the total labour force is not an important factor because the shares are comparable in Recife and Fortaleza (21%), yet the mean wages in those cities diverge sharply for the self-employed, moving significantly closer to the mean in Fortaleza and away from the mean in Recife relative to private employees. A similar argument can be made comparing Rio de Janeiro and São Paulo where the share of self-employed is 15.6% and 15.1%, respectively, but where the pattern of expected wages diverges considerably. Second, the wage level pattern for the self-employed has little to do with their personal characteristics. A comparison of the self-employed profile in Recife and Fortaleza shows that the divergent wage patterns between these cities are not matched by any comparably large differences in their demographic composition (see Chapter 2). A comparison of the self-employed in Rio and São Paulo reveals that the only significant difference in profile is that those in São Paulo are generally less educated, in contrast to their relatively high earnings. Furthermore, although the sectoral and occupational composition of the self-employed does seem to vary, the high degree of correlation between the self-employed group's expected regional wage levels with and without controls (0.97) indicates that the observed categories cannot completely account for the regional wage disparities.

The self-employed are a special category because, to some degree, they are not even a part of the 'labour market'. As Camargo (1989) points out, the earnings of the self-employed may be more strongly affected by conditions in their *product* markets than by specific labour market factors. The key reason for including them in the analysis is that self-employment can be a significant alternative occupation for those who have to labour for their income. It seems that the earnings of the self-employed are more heavily influenced by local product market conditions than by labour market factors. For example, the self-employed are largely involved in producing 'nontradeables' such as services or retail trade (ranging from 60% to 75% of the group). To the degree that regional product markets are favorable for the goods and services produced by the self-employed, their expected wages will be higher. The self-employed of São Paulo may do much better because they produce for a relatively affluent and dynamic local market. Those in Recife, by contrast, are crowded into such activities within a relatively poor and stagnant regional economy. In addition, differences in local 'nontradeables' will have an impact on all workers active in these sectors — whether they be self-employed or employees. This would account for some of the correspondence between the relative wage levels among the self-employed and private employees.

On the other hand, the greater regional wage dispersion for the self-employed could also result from systematic differences in motivation, skills, or resources which affect their earnings. Unlike employees, many of the self-employed have fixed or working capital and their earnings may then vary because of the returns to factors other than their labour power. Furthermore, self-employed activities are perhaps more responsive to individual initiative. Hence, the relatively high standing of the self-employed in Fortaleza could be explained by greater motivation or skill, while their peers in Recife are among the less motivated. It is difficult to measure or sustain such an argument, however, given the pattern which demonstrates strong contrasts between otherwise similar cities: Fortaleza and Recife in the Northeast, and even Curitiba and Porto Alegre in the south.

The magnitudes of the regional wage differentials for public sector workers are rather small, especially in comparison with the self-employed. When adjusted for estimation error, the adjusted weighted standard deviation[1] of their regional nominal wage differentials is only 4.5%. The relatively compressed wage gaps may result partly from federally mandated wage schedules for public sector employees, or from pattern effects in public sector wage negotiations. It is common for public sector workers to demand *isonomía salarial* (wage parity) with the Banco do Brasil employees — who are among the highest paid workers in Brazil. The 1988 Constitution specifically includes provisions for wage parity in public sector employment. Regional parity is an accepted norm in the public sector.

The results for private sector employees closely follow the results found in the entire sample, with personal and job characteristics both contributing to the reduction in the estimated conditional expectation of regional wage differences. Excluding the public employees and the self-employed, however, shows that job controls account for a larger share of regional wage dispersion among private employees (30%) than for the sample as a whole (20%). That is, the expected regional wage differentials for private sector employees conditional on sector and occupation are much less widely dispersed than the expected differential conditional on personal characteristics. The personal characteristics reduce the dispersion by some 7%; whereas the job controls reduce the expected dispersion by over 30%.

This result is especially interesting in contrast to the findings for the self-employed. For the self-employed, the dispersion of expected regional wage differences conditional on job characteristics is reduced by some 20% (from 0.281 to 0.225). The dispersion of expected differentials conditional on personal characteristics, however, is some 25% less (from 0.281 to 0.204). In contrast to employees, then, regional wage differences between self-employed individuals appear to result more from the regionally different composition of their personal characteristics than from their sector or occupation. This is not entirely unexpected. It is consistent with evidence that there are fewer barriers to entry by sector and occupation for the self-employed than for employees, and it confirms studies that show that the self-employed have widely varying strategies for earning income that are more closely related to their own personal characteristics than to a rigid sectoral or occupational category.

The standard deviations and estimated regional wage differentials for the public sector employees are barely affected by including job characteristics, which is expected because the sample selection effectively concentrates on one sector. It suggests only that occupational composition is not sufficient to counterbalance the unconditional expected regional wage differential. Nevertheless, personal characteristics can and do account for a significant amount of the regional wage differences (reducing the measured dispersion from 0.104 to 0.082), confirming conclusions by Macedo (1986) that education is an important correlate of public sector wages.

In combination with other information about the characteristics of wage determination among these groups, then, self-employed individuals display wage differences commensurate with the different composition of their own skills and characteristics and are influenced strongly by local conditions in their product markets. By contrast, public sector wages are regionally homogenous. The regional differences among private sector employees, meanwhile, is strongly influenced by the differing sectoral and occupational composition of employment opportunities across the major cities.

In terms of understanding the regional labour markets, this analysis has particularly highlighted the divergence between four extreme and distinct cities — Recife, Fortaleza, Rio de Janeiro, and São Paulo. Wages in São Paulo are consistently well above average in all cases, while the wages in the other three cities are consistently well below average. The major divergence in all four cases occurs among the self-employed, who fare relatively better than employees in Fortaleza and São Paulo and relatively worse in Recife and Rio. If, as argued above, this is taken as an indication of better market conditions in the product markets served by the self-employed in Fortaleza and São Paulo, then it indicates that São Paulo's other advantages in the labour market are shared widely — an indication of a strong dynamic regional economy. It also indicates that Fortaleza's economy is structured in such a way as to maintain substantial income earning opportunities for the self-employed in spite of the generally poor wage levels for employees. By contrast, Rio seems to have lost an important source of local economic activity with the federal government's move to Brasília and furthermore, no other economic activity — be it industry, commerce, tourism, finance, or self-employed activities — has expanded sufficiently to encourage dynamic growth. Recife represents a case where a poor regional economy leads to an overcrowding of individuals in sectors with poor earnings prospects. Unlike the self-employed of Fortaleza, the self-employed of Recife appear to have entered this segment as a last resort rather than as an opportunity for improving their incomes.

In sum, the findings in Chapter 5 of significant regional wage differences is not an artifact of combining heterogeneous categories of earners. *In no case was it possible to accept the hypothesis of no regional nominal wage differences.* Although significant and interesting differences exist among the privately, publicly and self-employed, the ranking of the regional wage differentials when estimated separately were broadly the same. There were significant differences between the groups, however, in terms of the magnitudes and dispersion of these regional differentials, as well as the relative importance of job or personal characteristics in accounting for uncontrolled estimates of regional differences.

Other samples and definitions

The robustness of the estimated regional wage differentials must be considered next in light of the earners who were excluded from the sample. This section will evaluate the robustness of the regional wage estimates to a variety of other samples and an alternative definition of income.

The estimates for several different samples and specifications are reported in Table 6.3 and show that the estimated regional wage differentials are robust. As above, the regional wage differences that are reported were estimated with regression (5.4) except where otherwise noted. Reporting the estimates from the other specifications would be lengthy without affecting the conclusions since the results from all four specifications are highly correlated.

First, similar regressions were done for women in order to see if the regional wage pattern was only apparent among men, or if the average wage differentials might be eliminated by a contrasting dispersion of women's wages. In fact, the regression for women strongly matched the ranking of regional wage differentials found for men. The regional dispersion for women, however, was significantly greater: 24.8% for the uncontrolled differentials and 21.9% for the controlled differentials. This confirms the hypothesis in Chapter 4 that excluding women from the sample would provide a lower bound estimate for regional differences in the labour force as a whole. Including women in the sample would have increased the estimated divergence in regional wage levels because the magnitudes of the regional wage differences are greater for women and the ranking simultaneously matches the ranking for the male sample. Note also that the addition of controls accounted for much less of the regional variance among women than it did among men, because the included variables do not account for as large a share of wage variation among women (see Table 6.3, column 1).

Another regression was estimated using income from all jobs instead of income from principal job because the incidence of multiple jobs might vary systematically across regions. Again the results were very close to those in the original specification in both ranking and dispersion (see Table 6.3, column 2).

Table 6.3
Controlled nominal regional wage differentials
for other specifications and samples, 1985

Metropolitan Region	Differences from Sample Mean (%)					
	Women	All Income	States	Migrants	Sectors	1985
Belém	-15.6	-9.6	-8.9	-49.1	-7.8	-10.0
Fortaleza	-42.5	-23.0	-28.6	-40.6	-22.0	-23.7
Recife	-49.8	-24.5	-23.8	-42.3	-20.0	-24.6
Salvador	-16.5	-6.2	-8.2	-17.1	-4.2	-5.9
Belo Horizonte	-13.4	-6.6	-15.2	-0.4	-6.4	-6.7
Rio de Janeiro	-8.0	-14.2	-10.7	-6.2	-12.9	-14.7
São Paulo	20.9	16.9	16.6	19.5	15.0	17.1
Curitiba	5.9	-0.8	-0.4	-3.8	-2.6	-0.8
Porto Alegre	9.0	0.9	-2.0	-6.4	1.0	0.8
Adj. Std. Deviation of Differentials	20.3	13.7	13.8	20.6	10.3	14.1

Notes: All of the reported differentials are from PNAD 1985 except for Migrants which drew from the 1977 sample. Women included female employees and self-employed workers in the nine metropolitan regions, and the same controls as used for men. All Income reproduced the results for the male sample using "income from all work", rather than "income from principal job". The "States" regression used a sample of male employees and self-employed residing in urban areas of the states corresponding to the nine metropolitan regions. The "Migrants" regression included two additional variables: a dummy for people who previously resided outside their current state, and time in years for those who immigrated.

Migration can be highly selective and might bias the coefficients. For example, São Paulo and Rio de Janeiro receive large numbers of immigrants who may have highly valued but unobserved abilities (Schmertmann 1988). To test the sensitivity of the estimates, a regression was estimated which included a dummy variable for whether individuals had been born outside of the metropolitan region, and another variable for their time of residence in that region.[2] The resulting estimates were not substantively changed (see Table 6.3, column 4).

Metropolitan regions are organized differently. In some, like Rio de Janeiro, many low-income neighborhoods (*favelas*) are located in the heart of the city; consequently, they are included within the Metropolitan Region. In other cities, like São Paulo or Curitiba, low-income population groups may be pushed to the metropolitan fringe and thereby reside outside the metropolitan boundary. In order to test the sensitivity of the results to the geographical definitions of metropolitan regions, a regression was estimated using all urban areas of the nine states which correspond to the nine metropolitan regions. The results show that the overall ranking is preserved and that Rio de Janeiro's expected wages, conditional on personal and job characteristics, remain some 10% below the national average (see Table 6.3, column 3).

In sum, over a variety of specifications and sample choices, the estimated regional wage differentials are robust. In light of the null models presented above, we can argue that nominal wage outcomes reveal regional differentiation in Brazilian labour markets which cannot be accounted for purely by composition effects — whether personal or job-related.

Conclusions

The hypothesis of no regional nominal wage differences has been rejected for a variety of specifications and sample choices. Estimated regional wage differences are significant after controlling for composition of the work force, in terms of education, age, and household status. They are also significant when adjustment is made for regional differences in the composition of jobs. The expected regional wage differentials conditional on personal and job characteristics are generally smaller than the unconditional expectation; that is, the regional composition does account for some of the regional divergence in wages. However, in two important cases (Rio de Janeiro and São Paulo) the adjustment for composition reveals a larger divergence from the mean. São Paulo's high wage level understates the wage advantage accruing to individual's with comparable personal and job characteristics. Rio de Janeiro's low wage level overstates the wage disadvantage faced by comparable individuals in that region.

The overall pattern of regional wage differentials which emerged from this analysis has the following characteristics. São Paulo clearly has the highest nominal wage level of all the metropolitan regions. Curitiba and Porto Alegre have comparable wage levels slightly above or near the sample mean. Salvador and Belo Horizonte are consistently some 5% to 8% below the sample mean in all the estimations. Fortaleza and Recife have wage levels consistently at the bottom of the scale, well below the sample mean. The estimates for Rio and Belém vary more than for other cities, and vary strongly in the case of Rio de Janeiro. Rio's ranking and relationship to the mean is the most sensitive to the choice of specification.

Disaggregation of the sample into public employees, private employees and self-employed showed that the broad pattern outlined above is maintained for the two former groups, while it diverges in important ways for the latter. Although the regional wage differentials for the self-employed differed significantly from the others, the hypothesis of no regional nominal wage differentials was easily rejected in all three cases. The results for the self-employed had little to do with their share in the labour force or the composition of this segment. Rather, the relative wage levels for the self-employed appear to indicate the importance of personal characteristics in determining their wages and also the degree of local economic dynamism which provides relatively good earnings opportunities in strong regions (São Paulo and even Fortaleza) and which depresses labour force earnings in others (Rio and Recife). In addition, estimated regional wage differentials for women, men in all urban areas, including all earned income, and including variables for migration status, confirmed the existence of regional wage differentials in a pattern broadly conforming to that described above.

The existence of nominal wage differences across regions which are not the result of observed work force or job composition indicates potential arbitrage on the *demand* side of the labour market. The divergence in nominal wages provides incentives for firms producing tradeable goods to relocate or expand in low wage areas. The nominal wage differentials also indicate potential gains for workers who migrate, i.e., potential arbitrage on the *supply* side of the labour market. The next chapter will investigate whether other factors counterbalance the regional nominal wage pattern for firms and workers. In particular, the estimated nominal wage differences will be discussed in terms of compensating costs of production as well as evaluated relative to regional differences in the cost-of-living and local amenities.

Notes

1. See Chapter 5, endnote 5, for a discussion of the adjustments to the estimated standard deviation.

2. This regression used 1977 data, the most recent PNAD survey which included information on previous place of residence. Subsequent surveys omitted migration-related questions until after 1988.

7 Cost-of-living, local amenities and compensating costs

Nominal wage gaps between regions may simply reflect regional differences in price levels or amenities which are faced by workers. They may also offset regional differences in costs of other inputs to production. This chapter analyzes these issues to show that the regional differences in wages are probably not a mere reflection of price differences or compensating differentials, and that opportunities for arbitrage are still apparent on the supply side of the labour market. On the other hand, it provides evidence that nominal wage differences do offset variation in complementary factors and productivity.

Can there be real wage differences?

The existence of differences in price levels is perhaps the most common explanation given for regional wage differentials, especially in a country as large and diverse as Brazil. It has been often argued that nominal wage differences merely reflect regional variations in the cost of living.[1]

This is a more complicated claim than it appears because local variation in price formation is also affected by local factor prices, including labour. Essentially, nominal wage differences can exactly reflect cost of living differences only under rigid conditions of isolated markets with comparable differentials in returns to other factors, or coincidences by which other factors offset the nominal variation in wages.

To formally analyze this question, a simple cost equation of the form

$$PQ = wL + rK$$

can be used, where:

P = price,
Q = quantity,
w = wage,
L = units of labour,
r = return to capital, and
K = units of capital

K can be considered capital or a combination of factors of production other than labour.[2] If Q, L, and K are relatively fixed, then we can differentiate this cost accounting function to yield:

$$\%\Delta P = \%\Delta w \; l + \%\Delta r \; k,$$

where l is the labour share of costs (wL/PQ) and k is the nonlabour share of costs (rK/PQ).

Previous chapters have shown that nominal wages vary by region, that is, $\%\Delta w \neq 0$. If we assume, in addition, that the factor shares of costs are the same in each region, then we can consider the three following cases:

1. *Closed economies.* By definition, closed economies are not subject to market forces that would lead to an equilibrium in any prices. In this case, the nominal wage differences could be exactly equal to the nominal price differences, if and only if the nominal rates of return for nonlabour factors were also exactly equivalent to the difference in nominal wages. By implication, real wage differences would be zero.

2. *Open economies with obstacles to factor flows.* In this case, product markets could function to equalize output prices, i.e., $\%\Delta P = 0$. In this case, the real wage difference would be exactly equivalent to the nominal wage difference. Implicitly, the returns to nonlabour factors would have to compensate as $\%\Delta r = (-l/k) \; \%\Delta w$.

3. *Open economies with obstacles to product and labour flows.* In this case, arbitrage in the nonlabour factor markets would eliminate differences in their returns ($\%\Delta r = 0$). Differences in product prices would then be a fraction of the nominal wage difference (i.e., $\%\Delta P = \%\Delta w \; l$). The real wage difference, then, would be equal to $\%\Delta w \; (1 - l)$. By inspection, as the labour share of costs declines, the real wage difference would approximate the nominal wage difference.

In Brazil, price variation between regions is largely due to variation in the cost of nontradeables (e.g., services, housing) since the prices of tradeables have been converging rapidly during the last thirty years. The returns to

93

nonlabour factors of production, probably vary significantly across regions,[3] but they can also vary between sectors. There appears to be some arbitrage in product markets as well as nonlabour factor markets. It is probable that the nominal wage differences overestimate the real wage differences and that price differences do offset the nominal wage differences to some extent. Given that the wage share of national production is estimated to be around 35%, the real wage difference would be approximately 65% of the nominal wage difference under the simplified model and conditions of the third case above. A regression of log wages on a price index, controlling for personal characteristics, estimated an elasticity of nominal wages with respect to price level differences of 0.61, which is significantly different from zero and from one at the 1% level. In sum, the above considerations suggest that nominal wage differences may overestimate the real differences in wages across regions by as much as 65%.

Given the lack of reliable evidence regarding the returns to nonlabour factors of production and regional input-output matrices, it is extremely difficult to evaluate empirically regional wage-price effects from the production side. The hypotheses necessary to undertake such an analysis would compromise the reliability of the results. Rather, it is necessary to explore direct evidence on price variation, even though such data are also weak.

Direct price comparisons

Direct price comparisons across regions in Brazil are extremely difficult because of the wide variation in consumption baskets. Beans make up a much larger share of family budgets in Fortaleza than in Porto Alegre, while meat products occupy a larger share of the family budget in Porto Alegre than in Fortaleza. Furthermore, the range of household income is so wide in Brazil that some manufactured and luxury products may be completely absent from the average basket of consumption in Belém, Fortaleza, and Recife, although they may be a significant part of costs for people in São Paulo, Porto Alegre or Rio. Furthermore, transportation and housing requirements vary significantly from the larger to smaller, and tropical to temperate, cities.

A worker's nominal wage should ideally be deflated by an index of the cost of living faced by that particular worker in his or her region, relative to the cost of living that would be faced by the same worker if relocated to another region. To do such an adjustment rigourously would require specification of the utility function for each individual or group of similar individuals, derivation of the corresponding price index, and data on the necessary weights and prices for each individual and region. Even if such were possible, it would be impossible to determine a unique index, since the choices of base weights for comparison — whether a particular region or a national average — are numerous.

In many countries, the choice of base weights would not affect the resulting indices materially. In Brazil, however, the choice of base weights is likely to yield widely differing estimates of relative inflation due to its high and accelerating rates of inflation. Only three authors have attempted to estimate price level differences: Thomas (1982), Rocha (1988, 1989), and Fava (1984). In each case, the same household expenditure survey data were used (ENDEF, conducted by the IBGE in 1974-75).[4]

Table 7.1 presents estimates of real wage differentials, using the nominal wage differentials which were estimated from equation (5.4) as applied to PNAD data from several different years. For example, the nominal wage differentials from 1985 in the first panel are the same as those presented in Table 5.2. Only Rocha's and Thomas' indices are used because the Fava calculations were the basis for Rocha's later work.

The Thomas index was used to adjust the nominal wage differentials for 1976. Thomas calculated this index by applying regional prices to an average national food basket and expanding it to incorporate nonfood items.[5] The index shows São Paulo and Rio de Janeiro to be the most expensive areas, while Fortaleza and Recife are the least expensive (see Table 7.1).

The measured price variation accounts for some of the nominal wage differences in 1976. Even after accounting for price level differences, however, the resulting real wage differences remain large and significant. The real wage level is closer to the sample mean than the nominal wage difference in six of the nine metropolitan areas, the exceptions being Belo Horizonte, Rio de Janeiro, and Curitiba. The ranking of the nine cities is the same with the exception of Belo Horizonte and Curitiba. Exceptionally low price levels and moderate nominal wage levels yield real wage levels for these two cities which are substantially above the sample mean. In Salvador and Porto Alegre, by contrast the real wage adjustment brings the wage level to the sample mean — i.e., the nominal wage levels in those regions can be largely attributed to price differences.

Table 7.1
Adjustments for differences in cost of living

Metropolitan Region	Controlled Nominal Wage Differentials (%)				
	1976	1981	1983	1985	1986
Belém	-51.6	-30.6	-22.0	-10.0	-22.8
Fortaleza	-52.5	-33.6	-29.1	-23.7	-26.5
Recife	-39.9	-28.5	-24.0	-24.6	-35.1
Salvador	-20.2	-7.9	-2.7	-5.9	-14.7
Belo Horizonte	-0.5	-2.5	-8.4	-6.7	-4.9
Rio de Janeiro	-10.7	-8.2	-10.9	-14.7	-17.1
São Paulo	22.4	16.0	16.6	17.1	22.6
Curitiba	-1.6	-4.8	-1.0	-0.8	0.6
Porto Alegre	-8.0	-3.0	-2.6	0.8	-3.5
Std. Dev.	24.0	15.4	13.3	12.2	16.2
Price Variation Across Regions (%)					
Belém	-2.3	7.9	12.6	10.1	30.8
Fortaleza	-23.8	1.4	-14.1	-21.2	-21.8
Recife	-17.8	3.3	-8.4	-6.0	-13.2
Salvador	-3.8	8.1	-3.3	-2.1	5.6
Belo Horizonte	-6.0	-10.1	-6.2	-3.9	-6.4
Rio de Janeiro	22.1	-1.1	4.2	12.8	-0.4
São Paulo	32.5	16.1	27.0	20.8	24.5
Curitiba	-7.5	-26.7	-17.4	-18.7	-22.0
Porto Alegre	6.6	1.2	5.7	8.2	3.1
Std. Dev.	16.9	11.6	13.2	13.4	17.5
Real Wage Differences Across Regions (%)					
Belém	-31.2	-27.0	-25.3	-12.5	-42.3
Fortaleza	-10.7	-23.6	-5.6	5.1	6.6
Recife	-4.0	-20.4	-6.3	-11.0	-10.7
Salvador	1.7	-4.6	9.9	3.8	-9.0
Belo Horizonte	23.6	19.1	7.1	4.8	12.8
Rio de Janeiro	-14.7	4.3	-5.8	-19.9	-5.4
São Paulo	8.0	11.4	-1.0	3.9	9.4
Curitiba	24.0	33.4	25.7	25.5	33.9
Porto Alegre	3.5	7.3	1.1	0.2	4.7
Std. Dev.	16.8	19.4	13.2	12.5	19.6

Sources: See text. Rocha indices used for all years except 1977 for which the Thomas index was used.

Overall the real wage levels continue to diverge significantly from the mean. Real wages in Belém are still 31% below the mean. Real wage levels in Fortaleza, Recife, and Rio de Janeiro remain some 4% to 15% below the mean. The wage level in São Paulo remains above the sample mean, if only by 8%. The dispersion of estimated real wages as a summary measure of the divergence of real wages from the sample mean remains significant with a standard deviation of about 17%, but may be largely driven by the dramatically higher than average real wage levels in Belo Horizonte and Curitiba.

Rocha's studies also use the ENDEF data to provide base weights for the indices. These studies differ from Thomas, however, in two ways. First, Rocha uses region-specific basket weights for the 20th percentile of family income to construct a region-specific poverty line. Her index is a measure of cost of living held constant by a caloric intake level which can be thought of as a proxy for constant utility. This index yields a price structure which is highly comparable to Thomas' price structure in some years (1985), and less so in others. Second, Rocha utilized yearly average food prices as collected by IBGE to construct the indices for later years through extrapolation.

Rocha's index also shows that price level differences are not capable of accounting fully for the nominal wage differentials. The real wage level in São Paulo appears to be high in 1981 and 1986, with real wage levels 9% and 11% above the sample mean. The estimates for 1983 and 1985, however, show the real wage level falling close to the sample mean. Recife and Rio de Janeiro have real wage levels which are quite low, as much as 11% and 20% below the mean in 1985, respectively. Using Rocha's index, Belo Horizonte does not have the dramatically high real wage level that resulted from the Thomas price comparison. Nevertheless, it does range consistently above the sample mean and close to or above São Paulo. The Rocha index also places Curitiba as the highest real wage area, with real wages some 25% to 30% above the mean. In 1985 and 1986, Fortaleza also comes out quite high, with real wage levels between 5% and 6%.

The ranking of real wage differentials, then, may differ from the nominal wage differentials in important ways. Workers in Fortaleza, Curitiba, and Belo Horizonte may earn substantially more in real terms than was apparent from the nominal wage estimates. On the other hand, the higher nominal wage level in São Paulo seems to overstate the advantage of workers in terms of their real earnings; the relatively low nominal earnings in Recife and Rio de Janeiro are not offset by lower than average price levels.

97

These estimates of real wage differences have two particular implications. First, they raise questions for studies which claim migration flows respond to income differentials. Areas which are typically considered to have low wages (in nominal terms) are expected to be sources of outmigration. After adjusting for price differences, however, some of these 'low wage' areas may actually have high real earnings. The data above suggest that there is little reason to expect workers to move in substantial numbers out of Curitiba to São Paulo, yet the number of people moving in that direction is substantially larger than the reverse (my own tabulations showed that 151,410 residents of São Paulo in 1977 had moved there from the urban areas of Paraná, including Curitiba, whereas only 35,373 residents of Curitiba had moved from urban areas of São Paulo). Similarly it would be difficult to explain substantial migration from Ceará (Fortaleza) to Rio.

Second, nominal wage differentials are expected to be mere epiphenomena, i.e., that real wages are equal and the nominal wages differ due to pure price differences. Although price differences are significant across regions, they do not appear to be large enough to account fully for the nominal wage differences. The rankings of the metropolitan regions are changed by the price adjustment, but the overall magnitude of regional differences is not greatly changed. The standard deviation of nominal wage differences is neither reduced nor increased significantly by the price adjustment: in 1983, nominal dispersion was 13.3% while the real dispersion was barely reduced to 13.2%; in 1986, nominal dispersion was 16.2% and real dispersion was 19.6%.

The greatest difficulty with these findings on real wage differentials is that they rely heavily on price indices which seem to vary significantly, and hence may involve significant stochastic variation or measurement errors. The following analysis tries to determine whether these estimates of real wage differentials are robust or whether they can be merely attributed to error in the price indices.

The analysis proceeds by looking at the magnitude of residual wage variation after attributing as much of the nominal variation to estimated errors in the price index as possible. The errors in the price index are themselves estimated under the extreme hypothesis that nominal wages are mere reflections of price differentials, in which case the wage-price elasticity would be one. In other words, by regressing nominal wage differentials on the available price indices, it is possible to evaluate the degree of price index errors and estimate real wage variation under the hypothesis of unit wage-price elasticities.[6]

To formalize the analysis, we can use the hypothesis that the true elasticity is one (i.e., that nominal wage differences are caused by price level differences), and estimate the implicit error in the price index with the formulas for bias due to errors-in-measurement.

Define the difference between the real wage in region r and the national average wage ($\hat{w}_r$) as

$$\hat{w}_r = \hat{\omega}_r - \Pi_r$$

where $\hat{\omega}_r$ is the estimate of the nominal regional wage difference as estimated in Chapter 5, and Π_r is the true price difference between the regional and the national average. If the real wage differences are only random and not structural, then the nominal wage difference ($\hat{\omega}_r$) is only a function of the true price difference (Π_r) and an error term:

$$\hat{\omega}_r = \Pi_r \, \eta + \zeta. \qquad (7.1)$$

The elasticity of the nominal wage to the regional price difference (η) can be estimated by regressing the wage differences on the true regional price index. However, the price differences are measured with error, so we must write:

$$P_r = \Pi_r + \upsilon \qquad (7.2)$$

as the relationship between the measured regional price difference (P_r) and the actual regional price difference (Π_r) where υ is a stochastic term measuring price index error. In a regression such as equation (7.1) which uses the imperfect price index (P_r) instead of the true price measures, the estimate of the elasticity (η') will be biased as:

$$\eta = \eta' \, (\sigma^2_\upsilon + \sigma^2_\Pi) / \sigma^2_\Pi . \qquad (7.3)$$

Knowing that the variance of the true price index is equal to the variance of the imperfect price index minus the variance of the price measurement error, and assuming that the true elasticity is one, we can calculate the implicit price measurement error as:

$$\sigma^2_\upsilon = \sigma^2_P \, (1 - \eta'). \qquad (7.4)$$

The estimates of the price error under the hypothesis of unit elasticity are shown in Table 7.2 for several years. In each case, the nominal regional wage differentials were regressed against an updated version of the Thomas index, utilizing annual inflation indices (INPC and IGP) of the IBGE.[7]

The standard deviation of the implicit price measurement error, assuming that nominal wages reflect price level differences with unit elasticity, ranges from 7.2% to 13.3%. The estimated price error is lowest for the 1977 data. The implicit error is greater for 1981 and 1985, where the hypothesis of unit elasticity is rejected easily by a t-test at the 5% level.

The final column of the table shows results from regressing the regional wage differentials estimated for 1977 to 1987 (excluding 1980) against the associated updated price index. In this case, the larger number of observations makes it possible to reject easily the hypothesis of unit elasticity. Since the early year (1977) is so strongly related to the (perhaps correctly measured) Thomas index, one might argue that the poor results in later years reflect a systematic problem in updating the Thomas index.

Table 7.2
Estimation of price measurement error and variance of real wages

	1977	1981	1985	All Years
η'	0.840	0.530	0.454	0.625
std(η)	0.269	0.179	0.195	0.058
t-statistic for $\eta'=1$	0.596	2.619**	2.800**	6.487**
degrees of freedom	7	7	7	88
R-Square	0.582	0.555	0.436	0.570
Under hypothesis that $\eta=1$				
Variance of Residual	0.029	0.017	0.016	0.015
Price Error Variance	0.005	0.018	0.016	0.013
Variance of Wage Error	0.0004	0.0004	0.0004	0.0004
Real Wage Variance	0.024	-	0.000	0.002
Std. Dev.	0.154	-	0.012	0.040

Notes:
1. Price index deflated with IBGE price indices (INPC and IGP).
2. The critical values for the t-test with 7 degrees of freedom and 5% significance level is 1.895. The critical values for the t-test with 88 degrees of freedom and 5% significance level is approximately 1.68.

Continuing with the hypothesis that nominal wages reflect price differences alone, we can estimate what the residual real wage variation would be. Under the assumptions, this real variation would be a result of

100

random fluctuation. The residual variation can be calculated as:

$$\text{Var}(\hat{w}_r) = \text{Var}(\hat{\omega}_r - P_r) - \text{Var}(\varepsilon) - \text{Var}(\upsilon),$$

where $\text{Var}(\varepsilon)$ is the variance of the nominal wage differential estimates (generally less than 0.0004)[8] and $\text{Var}(\upsilon)$ which is the estimated variance of the error in price measurement from equation (7.4). The resulting estimate for the standard deviation of real regional wage differentials is shown in the final row of Table 7.2.

For 1977, the adjustment yields an estimated regional dispersion of real wages equal to 15.4%, roughly comparable to the measured dispersion of nominal wages. Using the updated Thomas index for later years, however, suggests that real wage dispersion could be minimal — zero in 1981 and only 1.2% in 1985. Considering the entire ten-year period as a whole, the estimated real dispersion is 4.0%, considerably less than for 1977 and significantly smaller than for the nominal wage dispersion. It is possible, then, that the increasing integration of the Brazilian economy discussed in Chapter 3 has led to a narrowing of real wage differences across regions as of the early 1980s. This conclusion must be qualified, however, by recognizing that the implicit price error rises sharply, from 7.2% in 1977 to over 12% in the later years (a variance of 0.005 and 0.016, respectively). Hence, the low estimates for real wage dispersion could be an artifact of attributing greater measurement error to the price index when, in fact, the degree of error may be constant.

Real wage differentials, then, may have disappeared as of the early 1980s, but firm conclusions are not possible due to the degree of suspected error in the price indices. If on the other hand real wage differences exist, the degree of price measurement error makes it impossible to determine which areas lie substantially above or below the mean in terms of real wages. In either case, it is probable that real wage differentials are substantially smaller than nominal wage differentials across the major cities.

In combination with the simple cost model above, the real wage data also imply very different pricing behaviour across regions independent of nominal wage differences and in the presence of highly integrated product markets. This may reflect variation in market competitivity — regional segmentation of product markets being greater than suggested by the evidence — or a greater importance of nontradeables in local price levels.

Regardless of the explanation, the divergence between nominal and real wages has important implications. For example, it appears that social policy could encourage firms to relocate to Curitiba from São Paulo and thereby reduce nominal labour costs without reducing workers' welfare. This assumes, of course, that individuals would be better off in Curitiba with comparable real wages, ignoring other regional factors that affect well-being. It is entirely possible that even the small degree of estimated real wage dispersion reflects compensation for differences in quality of life. This issue will be discussed next.

Compensating differentials

If prices are not high enough in São Paulo to account for its higher wages, then are there other compensating differentials? Do people in São Paulo need a wage advantage to compensate for more pollution, congestion, and long commuting distances? On the other hand, people there also benefit from more and better public services, especially health and schooling. Do people in Rio stay in spite of lower wages because of its beautiful beaches? Then again, for the majority of the population living near the poverty level are such advantages worth accepting substantially less than obtainable in São Paulo?

It has been suggested that the wage gaps between these cities reflect compensation for quality of life or other regionally-specific attributes which yield nonmonetary benefits. It is difficult to argue conclusively that compensating differentials are insufficient to explain the entire real wage differential — or even to reverse it. On the other hand, the argument that compensating differentials do account for the wage gap must confront at least two issues.

First, individuals differ over how much they value region-specific features. Individuals will differ across regions because of the various influences of being raised in a particular area — family ties, information, and culture. Individuals will also differ over how they value things like public services and city life; and how they tolerate others like pollution, long commutes, and congestion. Therefore, the required compensating wage differential would reflect the amount of monetary compensation necessary to satisfy the marginal individual's preferences. This amount could be insignificant if there are sufficient numbers of indifferent people. Second, since regions have many facets, none fully dominant except in rare circumstances (such as hardship pay on oil platforms because of isolation), the pluses and minuses of a given region could easily balance, leaving no need for a compensating wage differential.

Rocha and Villela (1990) provide some evidence on the issue of regional amenities in Brazil's major cities, at least for the population below the poverty line.[9] Their study used the poverty line constructed by Rocha (1988) to delimit the poor population and then analyzed eleven indicators of living conditions for four separate years.[10] Their results indicate that, in general, living conditions are worse in areas with lower wages and larger shares of poverty. For example, Fortaleza and Recife have the highest shares of poverty and rank worst in terms of living conditions in all four years. São Paulo consistently ranks with the best living conditions for the poor, in spite of its relatively small share of individuals living in poverty. Curitiba is an interesting exception. It may have high real wages, as shown in Table 7.1, and a relatively small share of individuals living in poverty. Nevertheless, for those living in poverty, conditions were comparable to the cities of the Northeast in 1981, 1983, and 1986 (ranking 8th, 5th, and 7th for each year, respectively). Only in 1985 did Curitiba rank above the median (4th).

Confronting Rocha and Villela's ranking of living conditions for the poor and the real wage estimates in the previous section suggests that compensating differentials cannot explain the real wage gaps (see Table 7.3). Both nominal and real wage rankings are positively correlated with the living condition index (0.82 and 0.32, respectively), although the correlation between the real wage pattern and the living conditions index is not significantly different from zero. This comparison is by no means conclusive inasmuch as the quality of life ranking refers to a specific population subgroup which is defined with relation to the dependent variable in this study. On the other hand, the factors included in the index are city-wide indicators such as access to water and percentage of children in school. It confirms general impressions that regional amenities are not negatively correlated with real wage differences, and therefore, do not represent compensation for real wage differences.

Table 7.3
Comparison of regional wage differentials and poverty rankings, 1985

Metropolitan Region	Share of Population in Poverty	Living Conditions (Score)	Wage Differentials	
			Nominal	Real
Belém	43.8%	0.60	-0.100	-0.125
Fortaleza	36.6%	1.07	-0.237	-0.051
Recife	47.5%	1.23	-0.246	-0.110
Salvador	39.5%	0.57	-0.059	0.038
Belo Horizonte	36.1%	0.08	-0.067	0.048
Rio de Janeiro	36.8%	-0.63	-0.147	-0.199
São Paulo	26.9%	-1.88	0.171	0.039
Curitiba	24.3%	-0.22	-0.008	0.255
Porto Alegre	23.3%	-0.81	0.008	0.002
Ranks				
Belém	2	7	6	8
Fortaleza	5	8	8	6
Recife	1	9	9	7
Salvador	3	6	4	4
Belo Horizonte	6	5	5	2
Rio de Janeiro	4	3	7	9
São Paulo	7	1	1	3
Curitiba	8	4	3	1
Porto Alegre	9	2	2	5
Rank Correlations				
	(1)	(2)	(3)	(4)
Poverty Share (1)	1.00	-0.75**	-0.75	-0.63*
Conditions (2)	-0.75**	1.00	0.82***	0.33
Nominal Wage (3)	-0.75**	0.82***	1.00	0.65*
Real Wage (4)	-0.63*	0.33	0.65*	1.00

Notes: Share of Population in Poverty calculated in Rocha (1990) as share of population earning less than the poverty line income. Poverty conditions were scored in a multivariate principal component analysis. High scores indicate that those in poverty have worse living conditions. For example, high scores indicate that more people lack of access to water, sewage hookups, schools, and formal sector jobs. Significance levels indicated by asterisks as follows: * = 10% level; ** = 5% level; and *** = 1% level.
Sources: Poverty information from Rocha and Villela (1990). Wage differentials calculated by author.

Compensating costs in production: demand side arbitrage

The existence of nominal wage differentials which were estimated in Chapter 4 suggests that firms have incentives to move to or expand in the metropolitan regions with lower wages. Wages and labour costs, however, are only one part of businesses' total costs. It is possible that firms are uninterested in moving from their current locations because lower labour costs in certain regions are more than offset by higher costs of other kinds.

Hansen (1989) provides evidence for the state of São Paulo showing that wages decline as one moves farther from the centre of São Paulo, but notes that productivity advantages also decline by a comparable margin. Hansen estimates that:

> A doubling of distance from São Paulo City is associated with an 8.9% decline in plant productivity and an 8.7% decline in labour costs. Because of the slim difference between these figures, it appears that entrepreneurs can be indifferent in choosing where to locate their plant.

In interviews with businesses in Rio de Janeiro and Recife,[11] lowering labour costs was not generally considered a high priority relative to financial costs, input costs, and availability of public infrastructure. The low priority given to reducing labour costs was apparent from a surprising willingness to make wage concessions. This willingness to raise wages had various motivations. First, the interviewed business people were all willing to voice opinions that pay is abysmally low. Wages in Brazil are extremely low relative to costs of living. The minimum wage which was established in 1943 to support a typical working family is much less than that today. Second, labour costs were a small share of total costs for all firms, even those usually considered intensive in labour. For example, clothing manufacturers expressed as little concern for labour costs as the chemical firms which were interviewed. Considera (1986) argues that labour costs are a small and declining share of costs in manufacturing, falling from 20% in the 1950s to around 12% in the 1980s. Third, with high and accelerating inflation, conceding real wage gains today has little impact on real wages tomorrow. Inflation of over 10% per month with annual wage negotiations and quarterly wage indexation meant that real wage levels were easily and quickly eroded. By contrast financial costs are indexed daily, and input prices can change monthly, daily, or weekly, depending on agreements with suppliers.

In Rio de Janeiro, and especially Recife, the concern with nonlabour costs was apparent from the interviewees, preoccupation with infrastructure (water, energy, transportation) and financial costs. In several firms, self-sufficiency in terms of in-house generators, water storage, and repair shops was undertaken as an effort to insulate themselves from the poor provision of public infrastructure and local services. Every firm mentioned that cutting financial costs (and concurrently liberating cash for application in the profitable overnight market) was the key priority.[12] Reducing labour costs through moving or expanding elsewhere was not, therefore a key concern.

Although direct interviews were not conducted in São Paulo, several telephone conversations and discussions with visiting business people indicated the degree to which São Paulo's nonlabour cost advantages are seen as far outweighing its higher labour costs. In these cases, the business people talked about the difficulties of making interstate telephone calls, the importance of having their major suppliers nearby, easy access to key financial institutions, and the like. With low labour costs already, they were more interested in cutting major nonlabour costs and taking advantage of productivity gains in their current area.

Dependence of productivity on wages

In addition to compensating nonlabour costs, firms may be relatively insulated from market pressures if organizational and institutional factors are a more important influence upon their wages. This can occur whenever the wage level or pay scale affects labour productivity independently of the observable qualities of the workers who have been hired. Moving to lower wage regions in such a case would not reduce labour costs. The firm might have to pay the same wage regardless of location, or relocating might not yield savings in labour costs per unit of output due to reduced productivity.

In my interviews with Brazilian business people, certain firms used high wages as a strategy for improving productivity. It was not uncommon to find firms with an explicit policy of paying 25% to 50% more than the wage floor negotiated by the union and the employer's association.[13] Higher wages reduced turnover. Although training times were generally short, firms found the turnover in entry level jobs to be costly — in materials, time of training personnel, and the resources expended in selecting new employees. The greatest advantage of higher than market-clearing wages, however, was motivational: lower absenteeism, greater attentiveness, more effort. One informant argued emphatically that improving wages was the only way to improve labour productivity, but that such a policy must be accompanied by *conscientizaç ão*. The term comes from the popular movements connected to the progressive Church in Brazil

106

and indicates the process by which people become socially and politically aware. For this informant, however, the term signified making workers aware of the advantages the firm conceded *relative to other firms.* He planned to begin a monthly newsletter which, among other things, would regularly publish the difference between wage rates in his factory and those in surrounding firms. In addition, firms with high-wage strategies effectively improved their pool of candidates, frequently allowing them to attract workers who had developed their skills and become adept within smaller, lower-paying firms.

The high wage strategies were only found among large firms operating in protected markets — protected by brand names and product differentiation, or by government import quotas and tariffs. On the other hand, imperfect competition was not a sufficient condition for high-wage strategies. In several cases firms which adopted these strategies were otherwise indistinguishable from those which did not — whether in terms of their markets, technology, investment, or profitability. This was clearest in the case of two women's lingerie manufacturers. One followed a practice of paying at least 25% over the average wage level for seamstresses, while the other cut wages as sharply as it could. The former had few problems with workers, while the latter was being legally processed for subjecting employees to body searches — to make sure they weren't stealing the firm's products. In spite of these differences, however, both firms were equally profitable and expanding their production for both domestic and foreign markets.

These kinds of strategies vary systematically across regions. I encountered more firms in Rio de Janeiro which used high-wage strategies to improve labour productivity, reduce turnover, and improve applicant pools than I did in Recife. The literature on São Paulo indicates that the proportion of firms using such strategies is even larger (Morley 1979). When comparing the interviews, it was apparent that businesses in Recife were more polarized than those in Rio de Janeiro. The largest firms followed similar employment and pay practices as their peers (or parent companies) in the Southeast. Even among the large firms, however, there was much less interest in introducing labour management programmes. Most of the industries in Recife were content to let the Industrial Federation (FIEPE) represent them in labour negotiations, rather than deal directly with unions themselves. This was much less common in Rio de Janeiro.

An individual who was regularly involved in labour negotiations as an advisor and representative for industrial firms provided useful insights into geographical differences *within* the state of Rio de Janeiro. For example, in the cities of Nova Friburgo and Petrópolis where the industrialists are generally European immigrants or first generation Brazilians, this representative said the negotiations rarely end up in the labour courts — agreements are regularly reached with the unions without litigation. This indicates that the firms accept the bargaining process and use strategies which are less adversarial. In the city of Rio itself and in neighboring Niteroi, he characterized the firms as more belligerent, treating workers miserably, pushing the annual contract into the labour courts (a signal of intransigence), and regularly winning. The concentration of industrial plants around the steel complex of Volta Redonda are disposed to come to agreements, but face a much more highly mobilized and militant labour movement, and so have a mixed strategy of negotiation, bluff, and belligerence.[14] If business strategies vary this clearly across space within the state of Rio de Janeiro, it seems reasonable to expect variation across Brazil's regions, as well.

Consequently, firms are not highly sensitive to wages and labour costs in these major metropolitan areas. Although pay scales and wage levels are affected by local labour market conditions, wage policies contain provisions setting wages above what would be considered the market-clearing wage frequently enough to indicate important organizational and institutional influences on wages. None of the firms using such high-wage strategies indicated any desire to relocate in search of lower wages because the higher productivity associated with higher wages compensated for the higher hourly labour costs.

Conclusion

Real wage differences between the major cities of Brazil may have converged in recent decades as a consequence of the increasing integration of the national economy. Direct price comparisons and tests of real wage dispersion show that there may be real wage gaps between the major cities, but that these differences are probably substantially smaller than the nominal wage differences and may be insignificant. These findings, however, must be qualified because the accuracy of the price indices is notably poor.

Compensating differentials based on regional amenities do not account for the apparent incentive gap between the major cities. As shown by comparing real and nominal wage levels to an index of regional quality of life, higher nominal wages tend to be associated with better quality of life. There is no apparent relationship at all between estimated real wage levels and amenity levels.

On the demand side of the labour market, it appears that nominal wage differences are substantial and that they may be offset by compensating nonlabour factor costs. This has to do with the low level of wages, which make labour costs a small share of total costs, and the productivity advantages in certain regions (e.g., São Paulo) which may offset the higher wage levels. It also may indicate the degree to which wages reflect the organizational and institutional aspects of employment practices at the firm level which aim to increase worker productivity rather than market-clearing signals.

Notes

1. Thomas (1982) suggests that nominal wage differences themselves be used as an index of cost-of-living differences, discounting the possibility of real wage differences.

2. Intermediate goods are not considered for ease of presentation, but would not materially affect the conclusions. The assumption of constant factor shares across regions is important since arguments could also follow through the implications of changes in these parameters. For the purposes of this argument, however, the simplified presentation is sufficient.

3. Ablas (1985) presents evidence that rates of profit are much higher in the southeast.

4. The one exception is Rocha (1993) which utilized the more recent and less extensive data provided by the Pesquisa de Orçamento Familiar (POF), conducted by the IBGE in 1986, to construct updated region-specific poverty lines. This work arrived too late for incorporation in this study; however, a preliminary review indicates that the conclusions would remain unchanged by using this more recent index.

5. The expansion multiplied the basic food budget by the Engels' elasticities for people at the 40th percentile in the distribution of income.

6. The following discussion benefitted greatly from comments and suggestions by Kevin Lang.

7. The Thomas Index was chosen because it empirically explains more of the nominal wage differences than the other price indices. Thus, it provides a stronger test for the lower bound estimate of real wage variation. To ensure even greater accuracy of these statistical tests, the regional wage estimates were corrected for the log approximation. The indices used to deflate the price comparisons are discussed and presented in Savedoff (1992), Appendix A.

8. This can be found in Table 5.2, where the standard error of the coefficients is generally less than .02.

9. In 1985, this included about 33% of the population residing in Metropolitan Regions, varying from 23% in Porto Alegre to 48% in Fortaleza.

10. In order of importance, these indicators included piped water, informal employment, unemployment, sewage connections, garbage collection, underemployment, labor force participation rate, refrigerator, nondurable housing, proportion of school-age children who are working, and access to schools.

11. See Savedoff (1992), Appendix B, for a list of these interviews.

12. At the time of the interviews, *real* interest on government securities was approximately 30% per year (See *Conjuntura Econômica*, August 1989). In a context of high and fluctuating inflation, the spread between rates on borrowing and lending were extremely high. Hence, firms essentially sought to invest and finance themselves out of retained earnings. Any excess cash was easily, profitably, and safely deposited in the "overnight" accounts. When the Collor administration impounded the deposits in March 1990, many businesses were able "to liberate" their funds by using loopholes to pay off old debts with the "old" impounded currency.

13. Wages are generally negotiated between union and employers in a geographical area for a particular occupation or industry. The negotiated wage is considered a binding floor on contracts between individuals, firms and their employees.

14. The term belligerence is meant literally. The repression of workers was most severe under the military regime between 1968 and 1973. Nevertheless, as recently as 1988, federal troops killed 3 workers while trying to dislodge the union from its occupation of the steel factory in Volta Redonda. A monument to these workers was blown up in 1989, with the local military police considered key suspects.

8 Short term trends in regional wage levels

How are the regional differentials in 1985 to be viewed? Do they represent a temporary disequilibrium across labour markets in that year? Or if a permanent phenomena, why does anyone remain in a region where their earnings are as much as 15% or 20% lower than for a comparable worker elsewhere?

This chapter shows that the wage pattern in 1985 is part of a pattern which was relatively stable over an entire decade. It does this by estimating nominal and real wage differentials from PNAD data between 1976 and 1987. It evaluates the annual variations in this pattern in relation to measures of labour market slack and in the context of the macroeconomic trends of the period.

Nominal wage differentials, 1976-1987

An easy explanation for the regional wage differentials is that they represent a temporary imbalance or disequilibrium in the national economy. The normal flux of economic activity may increase and decrease the demand for labour in different regions from one year to the next. For example, a year in which demand for manufactured products surges will favor regions with a higher than average share of employment in this sector. Furthermore, over longer periods of time, birth rates, female labour force participation, and migration may change the composition and relative quantity of labour supply across regions. To test whether the regional wage differentials described above are a temporary phenomena, the

111

earnings function was used for each of the PNAD samples in 1976 through 1987 and correlations were calculated for each combination of years.

Table 8.1 shows the adjusted nominal wage differentials across regions for 1976 through 1987. In spite of the extreme changes in domestic growth and external trade experienced by the economy — from the recession of 1981-1983, through the recovery of 1984-1985, and the heterodox stabilisation plan of 1986 — the regional wage differentials are relatively stable. The unweighted correlations for 1976 through 1987 range from 0.78 to 0.99. They are all statistically significant at the 2% level. This stability is robust, holding even more strongly when using Spearman Rank Correlations. Correlations weighted by the different city sample sizes would be even stronger because the relative positions of the biggest cities — São Paulo and Rio de Janeiro — are very stable over the period. These high correlations across time make untenable the proposition that the regional wage differentials are solely a phenomena of short term market disequilibria.

São Paulo is consistently the highest wage area, with Fortaleza and Recife at the bottom of the scale. Belém, Recife, Fortaleza and São Paulo also show similar trends — converging toward the mean from 1976 until approximately 1984, and then diverging thereafter. Salvador, which in 1976 had average wage levels 20% below the mean, shows a steady improvement until 1983, and after that maintains a wage level only 5% or 6% below the mean except in 1986. The wage level in Belo Horizonte begins the period quite close to the sample mean and falls rather sharply after 1982. Rio de Janeiro shows the sharpest decline of all, with a peak of -4% in 1978 and a steady fall to -17% and -18% in 1986 and 1987. In 1976, the wage level in Curitiba is close to the mean and it falls until 1979. The wage level climbs steadily thereafter, reaching a peak of 3% at the end of the period. Porto Alegre mirrors Curitiba in the early period, diverging from the mean until 1979 and climbing thereafter. In 1986 and 1987, however, Porto Alegre suffers a sharp reversal, ending the period with a wage level some 10% below the mean.

Overall, there is no secular trend in the amount of regional wage differentiation for the period encompassing 1976 to 1987. The dispersion of the regional wage differentials declines from 21% in 1976 to a low of 13% in 1982, after which it climbs again until it reaches 20% in 1987. Every city experiences its minimum divergence from the mean sometime between 1983 and 1985, with the exception of Rio de Janeiro. Note that the sample analyzed in Chapters 5 and 6, using 1985 data, was among those with the lowest dispersion. Consequently, tests for regional wage differentials would hold even more strongly in other years.

The series is insufficient to determine trends, but it is interesting to note that the short term business cycle of itself cannot account for the observed variation in the regional wage pattern since years of growth (e.g., 1985) were comparable in dispersion to years of recession (e.g., 1982), while other years of both growth and recession had higher dispersion (e.g., 1978, 1986, 1987) (see Tables 8.1 and 8.2).

Looking at the decade as a whole, however, the pattern of regional wage differentials displays a U shape — with nominal wage dispersion declining into Brazil's deepest recession (1982-83) and climbing again after the recovery of 1985. Gomes et al (1985) document the staggered response of Brazil's major regions to the recession of 1982. They argue that the macroeconomic stabilization programme in 1982 affected São Paulo and the Southeast immediately by curtailing credit, reducing domestic demand for manufactures, and raising costs of imported inputs through the sharp devaluation. Later, in 1983 and 1984, the Northeast began to feel the effects of the credit shortage and input crisis, even while being relatively cushioned from the full effects of recession by continuing large government expenditures on personnel and employment. By 1984, however, the Southeast was beginning to recover, responding to the strong growth in exports encouraged by the lower valuation of the cruzeiro and other incentives. This staggered response to the recession can explain the compression of the regional wage dispersion in the mid-1980s, since it raised relative earnings in the northeastern cities at the same time that São Paulo reached its lowest point. Thereafter, as São Paulo recovered, the earlier pattern of wage dispersion reestablished itself.

Table 8.1
Controlled nominal regional wage differentials, 1976-1987

	1976	1977	1978	1979	1981	1982	1983	1984	1985	1986	1987
Belém	-52%	-50%	-40%	-40%	-31%	-26%	-22%	-13%	-10%	-23%	-26%
Fortaleza	-53%	-42%	-45%	-43%	-34%	-28%	-29%	-22%	-24%	-27%	-35%
Recife	-40%	-43%	-37%	-38%	-29%	-25%	-24%	-27%	-25%	-35%	-30%
Salvador	-20%	-18%	-16%	-12%	-8%	-11%	-3%	-5%	-6%	-15%	-6%
Belo Horiz.	-1%	-2%	2%	1%	-3%	-6%	-8%	-12%	-7%	-5%	-10%
Rio de Jan.	-11%	-6%	-4%	-6%	-8%	-10%	-11%	-14%	-15%	-17%	-18%
Sao Paulo	22%	20%	18%	19%	16%	16%	17%	17%	17%	23%	24%
Curitiba	-2%	-4%	-7%	-10%	-5%	-2%	-1%	0%	-1%	1%	3%
Porto Aleg.	-8%	-7%	-10%	-12%	-3%	-2%	-3%	1%	1%	-4%	-10%
Standard Deviation (Wtd. Adj.)	21%	19%	17%	17%	14%	13%	14%	14%	14%	18%	20%

Correlations

	1976	1977	1978	1979	1981	1982	1983	1984	1985	1986	1987
1976		0.99	0.99	0.98	0.98	0.97	0.93	0.81	0.82	0.90	0.91
1977	0.99		0.98	0.98	0.98	0.96	0.91	0.80	0.80	0.90	0.88
1978	0.99	0.98		1.00	0.98	0.95	0.91	0.78	0.81	0.88	0.88
1979	0.98	0.98	1.00		0.98	0.95	0.92	0.79	0.81	0.88	0.89
1981	0.98	0.98	0.98	0.98		0.99	0.97	0.87	0.88	0.92	0.93
1982	0.97	0.96	0.95	0.95	0.99		0.97	0.91	0.92	0.96	0.95
1983	0.93	0.91	0.91	0.92	0.97	0.97		0.94	0.94	0.93	0.98
1984	0.81	0.80	0.78	0.79	0.87	0.91	0.94		0.99	0.95	0.94
1985	0.82	0.80	0.81	0.81	0.88	0.92	0.94	0.99		0.96	0.94
1986	0.90	0.90	0.88	0.88	0.92	0.96	0.93	0.95	0.96		0.95
1987	0.91	0.88	0.88	0.89	0.93	0.95	0.98	0.94	0.94	0.95	

Note: All correlations are significant at the 1% level except 1984/78 and 1984/79 which are significant at the 2% level.

Table 8.2
Macroeconomic indicators for Brazil, 1976-1987

Year	Change in GDP	Industrial Production	Inflation
1976	9.0%	-	46.3%
1977	4.7%	2.1%	38.8%
1978	6.0%	6.1%	40.8%
1979	6.4%	7.0%	77.2%
1980	7.2%	9.1%	110.2%
1981	-3.4%	-10.2%	95.2%
1982	0.9%	0.0%	99.7%
1983	-2.3%	-5.1%	211.0%
1984	5.7%	2.6%	233.8%
1985	8.3%	11.9%	235.1%
1986	8.0%	6.9%	65.0%
1987	3.3%	-8.1%	490.4%

Notes: GDP using ECLA factor price method. Inflation measured by *Indice Geral de Preços*, from December to December. Industrial Production calculated from Industrial Production Index, *Boletim Conjuntural*.
Sources: Boletim Conjuntural, various years; and *Statistical Abstract of Latin America*, 1989.

The nominal wage differentials from 1976 to 1987 display both overall stability and important variations. The magnitudes of the nominal wage differentials are somewhat smaller at the end of the period than at the beginning, however, the trend from 1985 to 1987 is one of divergence. The cities at the extremes remain the same throughout the period: São Paulo maintains its position with the highest wage level throughout, while Fortaleza and Recife are always the lowest. The wage levels in Curitiba and Porto Alegre range close to the sample mean, but fall as much as 10% below. Salvador, Belo Horizonte, Belém, and Rio de Janeiro all range below the sample mean. Overall Salvador appears to have made substantial gains over the decade, while Belo Horizonte and Rio de Janeiro especially seem to have worsened. The high level of correlation indicates a consistency in the regional nominal wage vector across the entire period, and one which is comparable between the beginning and end years.

Real wage differentials

The evidence for real wage differentials presented in Chapter 7 shows that they may be fairly stable over time. Deflating the estimated nominal wage differentials by the available price indices showed real wage variation which is comparable to the dispersion of the nominal wage differentials (see Table 7.1). The resulting real wage pattern was shown to differ significantly from the nominal wage pattern, with São Paulo losing its first rank position to Curitiba, and Fortaleza displaying a real wage level close to the sample mean. These real wage patterns are fairly stable for the few years available as indicated by a high degree of correlation — ranging from 0.607 to 0.859, and all significant at the 10% level.

Unfortunately, the high degree of imprecision in price level comparisons brings the above findings into question. Under the hypothesis that nominal wage differentials fully reflect price level differences, it is possible to attribute almost all of the residual variation to errors in the price index in 1981 and 1985 (see Table 7.2). This approach indicates that real wage dispersion was significant in 1977 and comparable to the level of nominal wage dispersion. In 1981 and 1985, however, the estimated real wage dispersion falls close to zero. It appears, then, that real wage differentials may have substantially narrowed as of the early 1980s, but this conclusion remains tentative because of imprecision in the price data (see Chapter 7).

Short term changes and local labour market conditions

The rapid increase in dispersion between 1985 and 1986 merits particular attention in understanding the year-to-year variation. In 1985, the economy grew rapidly, 8.3% in real terms while industrial production expanded by 11.9% (see Table 8.2). This recovery which followed upon one of the country's worst recessions (1982-83) continued a pattern of inflationary growth which started in 1983. It was encouraged by continuing export growth, but also a boost in domestic government spending with the beginning of the first civilian regime in 21 years and a consumer boom. Inflation also accelerated dramatically, reaching 235%.

The regional wage differentials in 1985 are among the least dispersed for the decade under consideration. For example, starting with 1981 — a year of growth at the beginning of the decade — only Belo Horizonte, Rio de Janeiro, and São Paulo move away from the mean by 1985. Between the survey at the end of 1985 and that of 1986, however, every city moved away from the mean with the exception of Belo Horizonte and Curitiba. In 1986, the wage levels in the cities of the North and Northeast worsened, as did that of Rio de Janeiro, while São Paulo gained relative to the mean. This pattern in 1986 strongly resembled that of the 1970s, making the early 1980s look like a temporary phase of regional convergence. The regional wage divergence continued in 1987, showing that 1986 was not simply a one-year aberration.

On the other hand, there was every reason to expect that 1986 would have been the 'unusual' sample. In response to the high inflation of 1985, the government imposed a dramatic heterodox stabilization plan in February 1986 which froze prices, created a new currency, and raised real wages. As shown in Table 8.1, however, the net impact of these shocks was to reestablish the earlier pattern. São Paulo seems to have benefitted most from the year of heterodox stabilization, while the other cities dropped dramatically relative to the mean. Coming at a time when unions were less subject to direct military threats and repression, wages for many formal sector workers also increased beyond the official wage guidelines and it is likely that bargaining conditions were responsible for São Paulo's sharp gain in 1986. In fact, the wage gains negotiated by unions in the first half of 1986 represent a peak in real terms for wages over the past 4 decades, and were largely concentrated in São Paulo (DIEESE Bulletin, June 1986).

Table 8.3
Market conditions and regional wage differentials, 1985

Metropolitan Region	Average Unemployment		Annual Employment Growth		Wage Differentials 1985	
	1976-1986	1985	1976-1986	1985	Nominal	Real
Belém	5.6%	4.5%	4.3%	12.9%	-9.5%	-7.2%
Fortaleza	4.7%	5.2%	7.1%	8.1%	-21.1%	2.7%
Recife	6.7%	4.9%	3.6%	13.9%	-21.8%	-3.9%
Salvador	5.5%	4.4%	3.7%	9.8%	-5.7%	-1.9%
Belo Horizonte	5.7%	5.1%	4.5%	11.3%	-6.5%	-0.5%
Rio de Janeiro	5.1%	5.1%	2.7%	7.1%	-13.7%	-35.8%
São Paulo	4.8%	5.4%	3.4%	7.5%	18.6%	-13.8%
Curitiba	4.1%	5.0%	6.9%	8.4%	-0.8%	6.7%
Porto Alegre	4.3%	4.0%	4.1%	9.6%	0.8%	-5.8%
All	5.1%	5.1%	3.6%	8.4%	0.0%	0.0%
Correlations						
UE: '76-86	1.000	0.085	-0.462	0.770**	-0.493	-0.078
UE: '86	0.085	1.000	0.186	-0.316	-0.007	-0.134
ΔEmpl: '76-86	-0.462	0.186	1.000	-0.155	-0.188	0.724**
ΔEmpl: '86	0.770**	-0.316	-0.155	1.000	-0.401	0.336
Nominal Wage	-0.493	-0.007	-0.188	-0.401	1.000	-0.050
Real Wage	-0.078	-0.134	0.724**	0.336	-0.050	1.000

Notes: 1. Unemployment rate equals the number of people who reported not working and looking for work divided by the labour force in the PNAD household survey of the IBGE. The first column represents an average of the unemployment rates for 1976-86 as reported in Velloso (1989). The second column is the unemployment rate in September, 1985.
2. Employment growth refers to the increase in the total number of individuals who reported working as employees or as self-employed in non-agricultural activities in the IBGE's household surveys. The 1976-86 column is the average annual increase calculated from the endpoints. The 1985 column reports the increase from 1984 to 1985.
3. Controlled nominal wage differentials estimated with equation (5.4) and corrected for the log approximation. Real wage differentials deflated with the Thomas index.
4. Statistical significance of correlations: *** = 1% level; ** = 5% level; and * = 10% level.

Up to this point we have focused on the overall stability of the regional wage rankings. The existence of annual variation, however, suggests that wage differentials may also be affected by local labour market conditions.[1] In order to evaluate this hypothesis, Tables 8.3 and 8.4 below relate the wage differentials in 1985 and 1986 to two measures of local labour market conditions: the pace of employment growth and the unemployment rate in each metropolitan region. In 1985, São Paulo had the highest nominal wage level, but the second lowest real wage level.[2] In contrast to the high nominal wage level, or perhaps because of it, São Paulo had relatively low employment growth over the previous year (7.5% compared to an average of 9.8% for all nine cities). Furthermore, open unemployment in São Paulo was the highest of all (5.4%), perhaps accounting for the extremely low real wage estimate. On the other hand, Fortaleza had higher real wages than Recife despite its slower pace of employment growth and higher unemployment rate. For the cities taken together, the correlation between nominal wage differentials and unemployment is not significantly different from zero; and although the correlation between nominal wage differentials and employment growth in 1985 is negative (-0.401), it is not statistically distinguishable from zero as shown by a t-test. Hence, it is difficult to explain the nominal wage differentials in 1985 as a consequence of annual changes in local labour market conditions.

The pattern of unemployment rates and employment growth in 1985, however, were not strongly correlated with the historical trends. For the period encompassing 1976 to 1986, average unemployment in São Paulo was among the lowest, surpassed only by Curitiba and Porto Alegre. In 1985, however, open unemployment rates were lowest in Salvador (4.4%), Belém (4.5%), and Recife (4.9%). Similarly with employment growth, the rates of increase during the 1976-86 period are similar between Salvador, Recife, and São Paulo. In 1985, the rapid pace of employment growth was much higher in Salvador (9.8%) and almost twice as high in Recife (13.9%) in comparison with São Paulo (7.5%). Therefore, the absence of clear relationships between nominal and real wage differentials — which appear to be long term phenomena — and the rates of open unemployment and employment growth in 1985 may not be surprising. In fact, it suggests that the recovery in 1985 involved much more rapid growth of demand for labour in traditionally low wage cities than in high wage cities — hence reducing the dispersion of regional wages in that year. By contrast, economic expansion in 1986 was much closer in its spatial distribution to the historical trends of regional economic growth.

Table 8.4
Market conditions and regional wage differentials, 1986

Metropolitan Region	Average Unemployment		Annual Employment Growth		Wage Differentials 1986	
	1976-1986	1986	1976-1986	1986	Nominal	Real
Belém	5.6%	3.5%	4.3%	5.2%	-20.4%	-18.1%
Fortaleza	4.7%	3.4%	7.1%	9.5%	-23.3%	0.5%
Recife	6.7%	4.8%	3.6%	6.3%	-29.6%	-11.8%
Salvador	5.5%	4.7%	3.7%	-3.2%	-13.7%	-9.9%
Belo Horizonte	5.7%	3.3%	4.5%	6.7%	-4.8%	1.2%
Rio de Janeiro	5.1%	3.3%	2.7%	3.0%	-15.7%	-37.8%
São Paulo	4.8%	3.3%	3.4%	2.6%	25.4%	-7.1%
Curitiba	4.1%	2.1%	6.9%	15.5%	0.6%	8.1%
Porto Alegre	4.3%	2.7%	4.1%	2.0%	-3.4%	-10.0%
All	5.1%	3.5%	3.6%	3.7%	0.0%	0.0%
Correlations						
UE: '76-86	1.000	0.827***	-0.462	-0.261	-0.536	-0.275
UE: '86	0.827***	1.000	-0.461	-0.564	-0.485	-0.263
ΔEmpl: '76-86	-0.462	-0.461	1.000	0.776**	-0.089	0.743**
ΔEmpl: '86	-0.261	-0.564	0.776**	1.000	-0.045	0.537
Nominal Wage	-0.536	-0.485	-0.089	-0.045	1.000	0.279
Real Wage	-0.275	-0.263	0.743**	0.537	0.279	1.000

Notes: 1. Unemployment rate equals the number of people who reported not working and looking for work divided by the labour force in the PNAD household survey of the IBGE. The first column represents an average of the unemployment rates for 1976-86 as reported in Velloso (1989). The second column is the unemployment rate in September, 1986.
2. Employment growth refers to the increase in the total number of individuals who reported working as employees or as self-employed in non-agricultural activities in the IBGE's household surveys. The 1976-86 column is the average annual increase calculated from the endpoints. The 1986 column reports the increase from 1985 to 1986.
3. Controlled nominal wage differentials estimated with equation (5.4) using 1986 data. Real wage differentials deflated with the Thomas index.
4. Statistical significance of correlations: *** = 1% level; ** = 2% level; and * = 10% level.

120

Table 8.4 evaluates the regional wage differentials in 1986 relative to open unemployment and employment growth in that year. The most important result is the high level of correlation between regional unemployment rates in 1986 and their historical pattern, as well as between employment growth in 1986 and its historical pace, both statistically significant at the 1% level. In other words, the economic boom in 1986 which followed the heterodox shock of February 1986 reduced open unemployment in São Paulo and the South to levels lower than in the cities of the North and Northeast, as had been the historical pattern. It also resulted in a pattern of employment growth which, even though São Paulo remained low relative to the historical average, nevertheless restored the cities of the North and Northeast to more moderate paces of growth in line with their historical rates.

Although the spatial distribution of unemployment and employment growth in 1986 was closer to the historical pattern than in 1985, the estimated real wage differentials and the historical unemployment rates show the only statistically significant relationship. The correlation of -0.743, significant at the 5% level, indicates that where real wages are high, unemployment is correspondingly low. This has two implications. First, it may indicate that the real wage pattern is driven by labour demand growth in high wage cities, assuming that open unemployment is a good index for slack in the labour market. On the other hand, if the real wage pattern were the result of 'rigidities', e.g., wage strategies at the firm level which set wages independently of market conditions, it would indicate that migration does not generate pools of unemployed workers queuing for the privileged jobs. Open unemployment is always difficult to interpret in an environment with low absolute income levels and little public assistance since only individuals with substantial savings can 'afford' to remain unemployed while looking for work.[3] In this sense, unemployment is a better measure of slack among labour force subgroups with significant wealth, while wage levels themselves are more indicative of labour market conditions among poorer groups. Regardless, the evidence supports the view that real wages are higher in cities with traditionally low unemployment. It also suggests, although with less certainty, that nominal wages are also higher where unemployment is lower.

Employment growth is another index of labour market conditions, and its weak relationship to wage differentials is initially puzzling. The signs on the correlations for 1985 and 1986 all indicate that nominal wage differentials are negatively associated with historical trends in employment growth, but the correlations are not statistically significant. The evidence, however, indicates a positive and significant relationship between historical trends in the pace of employment growth and *real* wage differentials.

Specific estimation of demand and supply conditions would be required to verify these conclusions but this evidence, in combination with the evidence on unemployment discussed above, indicates that the pattern of wage differences are largely demand driven.

Conclusions

Nominal wage differentials are stable from 1976-1987, in the overall ranking of cities and in terms of the magnitudes of the wage differences, four categories can be distinguished. São Paulo stands by itself as the highest wage region, while a second group — Fortaleza and Recife — are consistently the lowest. A third grouping is comprised of Curitiba and Porto Alegre, which fluctuate near and a little below the sample average. A fourth heterogeneous group is composed of Belém, Salvador, Belo Horizonte, and Rio de Janeiro. The most significant annual variation is found in this group, with Salvador showing a steady improvement in its wage level while Rio de Janeiro suffers a steady decline.

Real wage differences may have substantially diminished in the early 1980s, but the price data are weak and the time period covered is too short for any conclusions regarding the responsiveness of real wage gaps to migration and labour supply shifts. Looking at the samples over time shows that the real wage differences may be increasing again in the late 1980s along with the divergence of nominal wages.

The observed movements in the nominal wage pattern appear to be driven by relative differences in the pace of economic activity when considering the impact of the 1982 recession and the later recovery which affected the Southeast first and only later had an impact upon the Northeast. More detailed analysis of indicators of labour market slack — employment growth and unemployment — showed a weak relationship between nominal wage levels and local labour market conditions; but estimates of real wage levels displayed a consistent relationship to the local market indicators — positively associated with historical employment growth and negatively associated with unemployment rates — suggesting that wage differentials are demand-driven.

The pattern of regional wage differentials is relatively stable over this short period, but is it of even longer duration? If so, what is its origin? Does it reside in the isolation of the metropolitan region labour markets? in the regionally-specific features of their sectoral composition or the quality of education? in the manner and process of contracting and utilizing workers in the workplace? The next chapter evaluates possible answers in light of longer term historical trends in labour supply, labour demand, and wage setting in Brazil.

Notes

1. See Savedoff (1991) for another look at this issue.
2. Recall that the price indices are subject to error and so the estimated real wage differentials are less reliable than the estimated nominal wage differentials.
3. Brazil adopted an unemployment insurance program as part of the Plano Cruzado in February 1986, however, it did not become effective immediately and so did not affect labor market conditions until later years.

9 Long term patterns of regional differentiation and integration

Regional wage differences are significant and persistent for at least the past decade. The previous chapter showed tentative evidence that annual variations in the regional wage pattern may be related to changes in local labour market conditions. This chapter seeks to extend this analysis further by considering the last four decades. First, evidence will be shown on the persistence of regional wage differences over the period 1950-1980 using two additional data sources. Then, the various explanations for regional wage differences will be evaluated in light of this persistence as well as the long term trends in labour supply, labour demand, and overall economic integration discussed in earlier chapters. Finally, the chapter will draw together the information into a coherent explanation for the observed pattern of regional wage differences.

Long term stability: 1950-1980

Although the household survey data are only available for the past decade and a half, at least in the case of nominal wages it is possible to test the stability over a longer period using other sources. This section focuses on two such sources: the IBGE's Industrial Census and Demographic Census.

The Industrial Census of Brazil allows one of the longest series of regional wage comparisons, from 1949 to 1980. The textile industry was chosen for analysis because a sizable sample of firms existed in each of the selected states and because it provides some control for worker quality due to the relative homogeneity of skills in its production tasks. The industrial census provides data on the total wage bill for production workers by industry and state along with the total number of employed production workers. The average wage per production worker was calculated from this data as a proxy for average wages. The usefulness of the proxy should by qualified since it implicitly assumes that variation in individuals and in hours worked across regions does not contribute significantly to the observed regional differences.

Table 9.1
Regional wage differentials for textile industry workers

| | Differences in average wage from sample mean for production workers (%) | | | |
	1949	1959	1970	1980
Pará	-57.1	-26.2	-31.9	-41.2
Ceará	-49.8	-49.2	-50.3	-48.3
Pernambuco	-32.4	-31.5	-27.7	-13.3
Bahia	-23.6	-25.1	-36.0	-15.6
Minas Gerais	-32.7	-19.8	-25.5	-25.7
Rio de Janeiro	5.9	10.9	-1.3	-1.3
São Paulo	13.3	7.0	10.4	12.0
Paraná	-32.4	-20.4	-2.6	-12.2
Rio Grande do Sul	6.8	4.4	-11.5	-14.9
Wtd. Std. Dev.	8.8	5.6	7.2	7.9
Mean Wage (Cr$)	9,761	64,658	116,953	96,087

| Temporal Weighted Correlations (N = 9) | | | | |
	1949	1959	1970	1980
1949	1.00	-	-	-
1959	0.97	1.00	-	-
1970	0.96	0.88	1.00	-
1980	0.93	0.85	0.99	1.00

Note: All correlations are significant at the 1% level.
Source: Calculated from IBGE, Industrial Census.

The findings, shown in Table 9.1, are nonetheless striking. From 1949 through 1980, the industrial census shows highly correlated regional wage differentials. The lowest correlation between any two years, 0.85 for 1959 and 1980, is still highly significant, passing a t-test at the 1% level. The dispersion of regional wage differentials in textiles declines from 0.088 to 0.056 in 1959, but the subsequent period — a period of very rapid economic integration — shows an increase in regional dispersion to 0.072 in 1970 and again to 0.079 in 1980.

The data show that in 1949 textile workers earned above the sample average in the states of São Paulo, Rio de Janeiro, and Rio Grande do Sul (Porto Alegre). The textile workers in Bahia earned some 24% less than the average, while those in the remaining four states (Pará, Ceará, Pernambuco, and Paraná) had earnings which were 30% below the mean or lower. Rio Grande do Sul declines steadily over the four decades, while Paraná which is also in the nation's South, experiences a comparable increase in wage level. Bahia and Recife have substantial increases in textile workers' average earnings between 1970 and 1980, while Rio suffers a substantial decline over the same period. São Paulo maintains its high standing throughout the period, suffering a decline between 1949 and 1959, but increasing farther above the mean in the two decades which follow. Pará remains very far below the mean throughout the period, with some improvement, as does Minas Gerais.

A similar analysis was undertaken using the Demographic Censuses of 1960, 1970 and 1980. The results (see Table 9.2) show a similar stability of regional wage differentials. In this case, the data were obtained for men with four years of schooling in each of the nine states. The pattern is highly correlated across all three censuses. The dispersion increases between 1960 and 1970 from 0.137 to 0.173 and declines slightly to 0.152 in 1980.

The two data sets show fairly similar trends for the 1960s, but diverge substantially between 1970 and 1980. This is not unreasonable given that the data sets are 'controlled' in different ways: the remunerative value of schooling has certainly changed over time, as has the character of the textile industry in terms of technology, products, markets and organization. Secondly, the state averages from the demographic census are also affected by the differing rural shares of population, whereas the average wages calculated from the industrial census probably exclude rural residents. Finally, the industrial census data involve a smaller base of observations, and hence could easily be skewed by a few large firms in any particular state. In spite of the problems in comparability, however, the degree of consistency between the two samples for particular cases is of great interest.

126

Table 9.2
Regional wage differentials for men with four years of education

	Difference from Mean (%)		
	1960	**1970**	**1980**
Pará	-27.3	-34.8	-17.0
Ceará	-30.9	-36.4	-29.6
Pernambuco	-35.2	-26.8	-29.5
Bahia	-29.3	-24.5	-9.8
Minas Gerais	-11.9	-18.5	-14.8
Rio de Janeiro	6.8	-1.0	-4.9
São Paulo	10.9	15.0	18.6
Paraná	-1.9	-11.7	-7.3
Rio Grande do Sul	-19.5	-28.7	-5.5
Wtd. Std. Deviation	13.7	17.3	15.2
Mean Wage (Cr$)	9,447	344,900	3.17 Min. Wages

Temporal Correlations (N = 9)			
	1960	**1970**	**1980**
1960	1.00	-	-
1970	0.94	1.00	-
1980	0.90	0.94	1.00

Note: All correlations are significant at the 1% level. Mean wages are reported in current cruzeiros, except for 1980 which is reported relative to the minimum wage.
Source: Calculated from IBGE, Demographic Census.

For example, the census data confirm São Paulo's persistently high nominal wage level and shows that this advantage grew consistently through the two decades. This data also confirm Rio de Janeiro's declining relative wage level (from 7% above the mean to 5% below), and Salvador's significant gain (from 29% below the mean to 10% below the mean). It also confirms the persistently low nominal wage levels in Fortaleza (Ceará) and Recife (Pernambuco).

The data sets diverge in particular instances, especially for the 1970s. The census data show a climb in Pará's wage level from 1970 to 1980 which is not reflected in the data on textile workers. By contrast, the demographic census data show no signs of the wage gains in Pernambuco that apparently affected textile workers in that state between 1970 and 1980. The relative wage levels in the two southern states, Paraná and Rio Grande do Sul, converge toward each other in both data sets, but in the census data Paraná begins close to the mean and falls, while in the textile industry data it starts well below the mean and climbs. Rio Grande do Sul exhibits almost the exact reverse.

The evidence, then, suggests that regional wage differences are a recurring phenomena, but one that changes within certain ranges. In data sources, the state of São Paulo is shown to be the leading high wage area. The states of Pará, Ceará, Pernambuco, and Minas Gerais are all below the national average, which is consistent with the evidence from the recent decade presented in Chapter 8. The evidence for Bahia, heavily influenced by Salvador, its capital city, shows the remarkable improvement in relative wage levels between 1970 and 1980 in both the demographic and industrial census data, while Rio de Janeiro is confirmed to be suffering a secular decline, beginning in 1960 when the federal capital was officially moved to Brasília. The evidence is less consistent with the earlier data for the southern states of Paraná and Rio Grande do Sul.

Explanatory factors: labour supply, labour demand, transaction costs, and institutions

If there is a discernible pattern from the 1950s onwards, how is it to be explained? The historical trends discussed in Chapter 3 have a bearing on the persistent regional wage differentials since they involve the spatial dispersion of the labour force and its quality; the pattern of job opportunities and their related productivity; the degree and pace of economic integration; as well as trends in public policy, union activity, and firm-level strategies. It is worth reviewing these trends to consider which are more related to the persistence of regional wage disparities, and the deviations from the overall pattern.

Could labour supply be persistently expanding faster in certain areas and thereby provide continual pressure to lower wages? As discussed earlier, population growth and migration have contributed substantially more to labour force growth in São Paulo over the entire period than in any other area. Since São Paulo has consistently higher wages, labour supply does not seem to be of direct importance. In other cases, Rio de Janeiro and

128

Recife in particular, the paces of labour supply growth are fairly rapid and are associated with low wage levels. Rapid supply growth may be necessary but it is not sufficient to explain low wage levels in certain regions.

Could there be systematic differences in labour force quality which make firms willing to pay workers more in particular regions? The differences in educational levels seem to be converging over the long run, even though this trend is less evident in the past decade. The trends in schooling, however, are not apparently central to the regional wage differences, which do not show a comparable convergence over the lengthy period considered.

In addition, interviews found little evidence of systematic differences in labour quality. In both Rio de Janeiro and Recife, employers stated that training times were quite short for all their positions. Workers generally met employers' standards within two weeks to three months, depending on the product, technology, and position. Consequently, although firms in Recife complained much more about labour quality, their own admission of fast and easy training suggests that worker trainability was generally sufficient for the tasks involved.

Could different regional paces of employment growth and labour demand account for the persistent regional wage differences? Direct confrontation of historical paces of employment growth and unemployment with regional wage differentials suggested that local labour demand plays a role in determining relative wage levels, and the historical data on the spatial pattern of economic growth are significantly related to the pattern of regional wage differentials. In this sense employment growth and labour demand may explain a large part of the regional wage differences.

São Paulo's consistently high wages are matched by its rapid growth in economic activity which allowed it to maintain its share of national output and industrial production throughout the last few decades. The continuing concentration of industrial activity in São Paulo is the strongest example of a region-specific advantage, and one which is remarkable given the potential savings in labour and land costs from moving out of Greater São Paulo. The consistent spatial concentration of industry, due to agglomeration economies, public infrastructure, and interactions with available labour pool skills, is the regional pattern most closely related to the observed pattern of regional wage differentials.

The labour demand patterns seem to account for the major exceptions to the historical persistence of regional wage differentials, as well. Salvador's improving wage level occurs during the 1970s, exactly when public investment dramatically expanded industrial output and industrial capabilities in Salvador. Rio's declining share of economic output and falling relative wage level occurs in concert with the transfer of the federal government.

In addition to the impact of economic activity more generally, could there be region-specific factors that affect labour productivity? Information from interviews and studies of business in Brazil show that firms encounter cost advantages in certain areas. There is insufficient information however to determine whether this productivity is specific to technologies, sectors, or agglomeration economies. Regional wage differentials are highly correlated with data on labour productivity in manufacturing, with the exception of Rio de Janeiro. It is difficult, however, to decompose these productivity differences into region-specific and nonregion-specific categories.

Could there be significant transaction costs and/or obstacles to factor price equalization? This is unlikely because the rapidity of economic integration in the past few decades has reduced a variety of transaction costs, both informational and physical, without any apparent comparable reduction in regional wage dispersion. This economic integration has made it possible for firms to maintain access to financial markets throughout the country, to ship products nationally, and to communicate with dispersed offices. It has also made it easier and less costly for workers to migrate, whether permanently or temporarily, as well as making available a great deal of information about jobs, income, and living conditions in distant places. Real wage differences could be converging in association with the increasing integration, as was suggested by evidence in Chapter 7. On the other hand, a significant convergence of real wages along with the apparent persistence of nominal wage differentials would require price level differences to be diverging — a proposition which is not supported by evidence in recent price surveys (Almeida 1992, Rocha 1988, IBGE data). The regional wage differences do not result from a static equilibrium with 'wedges' driven between regional price and wage levels by transaction costs since such costs have been declining at a time when regional wage levels persist. It is therefore very difficult to claim that the regional wage differences are an artifact of geographic obstacles or price differences.

Could government policy have contributed significantly to the persistence of regional wage differences? To the degree that government wage policies have been effective, they have worked toward reducing regional wage disparities. The persistence of regional wage differences through a period when government mandated minimum wages were converging to a national standard suggests that this policy did not significantly influence the regional wage differences. Government wage policies do not seem to account for the regional differences, although the policies of national wage indexation may have encouraged original wage differences to persist.

130

Could regional differences in union activity account for the regional wage differences? Union activity may strongly influence wages in Brazil, however, such activity has been highly variable over time as a result of political change and military repression. Union strength cannot account for São Paulo's continuing wage advantage since the 1950s because for almost two decades (1964-1978) the workers movement was effectively stifled.[1] Although the labour movement is an essential part of Brazilian economic and political history, it cannot by itself be the key to the persistence of regional wage differentials.

Finally, could firm-level strategies of employment and pay generate regional wage differences? It is possible for equally profitable firms to coexist in the same markets and follow different wage strategies as was found in various interviews. If certain regions had proportionally more firms following 'high wage' strategies, in which they pay wages above market-clearing levels but are compensated by greater labour productivity, then regional wage differences could occur even in the presence of factor flows because the resulting job opportunities would be rationed.[2] Unfortunately there is too little evidence to evaluate the impact of these firm-level strategies on labour market operation, whether in cross-section or over time.

Conclusions

It appears that Brazil has a strongly integrated national economy, but one which nonetheless continues to generate significant nominal wage differences, and perhaps real wage differentials as well. The persistence of these differences is sustained by tight labour market conditions in high wage areas and weak conditions in low wage areas which have been reproduced through Brazil's specific process of spatial economic development. This section discusses the patterns which stand out as essential to explaining regional wage differences.

First, the metropolitan regions do not appear to be isolated in terms of the labour market and wage determination. Economic integration increased over the period, as shown by evidence on communications, transportation, convergence of prices for consumer durable goods, interstate commerce, and migration. The costs of migration have been declining and the pace of migration is very large relative to the labour force. The magnitudes of labour flows are so large that only a rapid pace of expanding labour demand or intraregional segmentation of job opportunities could account for the absence of factor price equalization. Geographic obstacles *per se* are not apparent. There are also large product flows, so that factor price equalization cannot be impeded by constraints on specialization in products intensive in the local abundant factors.

The one relevant market that shows signs of immobility is capital. Capital does not seem to move except with strong and costly public incentives (e.g., SUDAM, SUDENE, Camaçarí, etc.). This is consistent with the existing private incentives which encourage production in the Southeast and especially in São Paulo due to agglomeration economies and access to infrastructure and markets. The low share of labour costs, even in São Paulo, means that firms have little incentive to seek lower wage areas except in rare circumstances. [3]

The resulting industrial concentration, for example, is the most stable aspect of spatial differences between 1950 and 1980. This may indicate that the degree of capital immobility described in earlier chapters reproduced dynamic conditions of labour demand growth, sufficient to absorb labour force increases in some areas and sustain higher wages, while being insufficient to absorb labour force increases in other areas. Regional variation in productivity matches this concentration in its stability over time. Only in Bahia were there substantial productivity gains in the 1970s.

Demographic trends and migration patterns have continued to reproduce the same labour supply conditions across regions during this period. Labour supply has continued to grow at a remarkable pace of over 5% annually in all of the metropolitan regions. This stems largely from natural increase, but the boost from migration is significant, steady, and predominantly composed of working age people. São Paulo and Rio de Janeiro continue to have the greatest growth in labour force throughout the period since 1950, although this growth began to decelerate in Rio in the 1970s.

Combining the stability of labour force growth with the stable pattern of industrial concentration and productivity suggests that wage differentials could be continually reproduced through this period by the parallel dynamic of labour supply growth and labour demand increase. In other words, labour force growth was fast enough to persistently outstrip employment growth in the Northeast and Rio, while São Paulo has continued to grow and absorb workers almost as fast as its 100,000 annual migrants can arrive.

The complete picture, then, shows that regional wage differences are driven in the long term by a pattern of spatial economic growth which is concentrated and most dynamic in São Paulo. The effect of this long term pattern on wages is reinforced by cost advantages to firms in São Paulo which encourage them to remain and expand within São Paulo, and secondly, by demographic trends and migration which depress wages in slower growing cities but which are absorbed by São Paulo.

The exceptions to this rule deserve some special attention. First, Rio de Janeiro shows that being first is not sufficient for continuing prosperity. Rio was a dynamic growth centre, attracting migrants and paying high wages until its economic structure was seriously changed by the federal government's move to Brasília. Since 1960, there appears to be a sizable inertia in migration to Rio despite a steadily declining relative wage level. In addition, no other economic sector has grown substantially to replace the large loss of public employment.

Second, Salvador shows that the regional wage differences are not immutable and can also be influenced by government policy. Labour productivity and wage levels in Salvador rise significantly from the mid-1970s into the 1980s. The timing coincides directly with public investment in infrastructure for the petrochemical pole and other related industrial parks. The most interesting finding in this case is that the impact of this massive investment was not confined to wages in the industrial sector. Rather, the impact on wages was generalized, even raising the relative wage level of domestic servants.

Fortaleza and Recife show the importance of distinguishing different segments of the labour force by employment status. Although both cities have substantially lower nominal wages than any other region, the self-employed in Fortaleza enjoy relatively higher wages than their employed counterparts while those in Recife do relatively much worse. This divergence indicates that there are regional differences in local product markets and economic organization which have a significant impact on incomes but which are not captured by the standard variables employed in household surveys. These two cities also show the importance of obtaining better and more reliable price data since the available price data suggest that Fortaleza's labour force may be paid higher than the sample mean in real terms while real wages in Recife could be substantially below the sample mean. The high degree of error in the price indices, however, make this proposition very tentative.

Regional wage differentials in Brazil's urban labour markets are therefore the result of a process of regional development which has reproduced relatively tight market conditions in certain areas — notably São Paulo — and weak market conditions elsewhere — notably Recife and Fortaleza. This conclusion must be qualified, however, by recognizing other explanations which cannot be strictly ruled out at the present time. First, it is still possible that there are unobserved differences in workers that affect productivity, vary systematically across regions, and are not correlated with the observed variables of personal characteristics which

133

were used in this study. The robustness of the regional wage differentials to the inclusion of personal characteristic variables which capture some 50% of log wage variance, however, suggests that further information about personal characteristics would not be likely to affect the regional wage difference estimates substantially.

Second, the sectoral variables which were used could not capture the full range of productivity differences among firms because the sectors are highly aggregated. This masks compositional differences that also vary systematically across regions. The interviews and literature on firms in Brazil suggest that wage-setting strategies may vary systematically across regions and therefore that regional wage differentials could be driven by these institutional 'rigidities'. That is, efficient organizations may systematically differ across regions in the way they use wages and nonwage factors to organize and mobilize productive labour.

Thirdly, compensating differentials were shown to be unlikely as an explanation for the regional wage differentials because of the positive correlation between living conditions and real wages. The statistical test was suggestive, and not absolute proof, of this positive relationship. On the other hand, different measures of living conditions might show regional amenities to be a more important factor; or additionally, labour force subgroups may sort themselves along different dimensions by which they value regional amenities.

Most importantly, the explanation of regional wage differentials as a consequence of persistently reproduced labour supply and demand conditions leaves aside important issues of historical context. Why is it that one region develops a dynamic growth rate which outpaces labour supply while others do not? What are the political and social histories which lead to particular forms of organizing labour and concentrating capital and wealth? What local conditions could affect the range of income-earning opportunities for labourers and explain the different wage levels of self-employed workers, as in, for example, Recife and Fortaleza? The persistence and significance of regional wage differentials in Brazil reflect its particular pattern of spatial economic development, but fully understanding this pattern requires more detailed comparisons of the regional economies.

Notes

1. After the military coup of 1964, the number of strikes fell to virtually zero in the following three years. Major strikes in 1968, beginning in Osasco, were severely

repressed. Only after the 1978 strike wave did the labor movement resume an active and visible role.

2. Such firm-level strategies would only result in persistent regional wage differences if workers were well-informed of job opportunities in all regions and did not migrate until jobs were available. Otherwise, queuing could still drive down expected wages in a region which had proportionally more "high-wage strategy" firms.

3. In this regard, consider the debate starting with Storper (1984).

10 The meaning of regional wage differentials in Brazil

Brazil is not the same country that it was only thirty or forty years ago. In a relatively short time, it ceased to be a predominantly rural agro-export economy and instead became urban and industrial. In the same period it experienced years of both civilian and military rule, and was subjected to a range of national development policies with varying regional impacts. From being an 'archipelago' of relatively isolated regional markets, it became more economically integrated, with interstate trade expanding faster than the remarkable 7% annual growth of GDP.

The evidence of persistent regional wage differentials presented in this study, then, is surprising. The wage gap between major urban areas continues through several decades in spite of ample geographic mobility of labour and product market integration. The only key market which did not show great mobility was physical capital. This is perfectly comprehensible given the high profit rates in the areas of existing industrial concentration aided by infrastructure, proximity to major markets, and low labour costs. The mobility of labour and products, however, would generally be sufficient to erase arbitrage opportunities across these metropolitan regions in most market models. The answer to the persistence of regional wage differentials lies in the reproduction of relative differences in labour market conditions due to the remarkable inertia of regional differences in productivity growth and industrial concentration, and large but lagging supply responses. Returning to the framework presented in Chapter 1, it is now possible to evaluate the explanations for regional wage differences as reflecting variation in productivity, price and compensating differentials, or rents.

Explaining regional wage differentials in Brazil

In the case of Brazil's metropolitan regions, there are productivity differences which have persisted over the period of analysis. The different composition of labour force quality and labour demand, however well they explain individual variations in earnings, do not explain the regional disparities as shown by the independence of the estimated wage gaps to the inclusion of these factors in the earnings functions. Instead, *social* productivity must account for much of the regional differential. In other words, agglomeration economies, infrastructure, production externalities, on-the-job-training, and the development of specific skills have created, and recreated, disparities in productivity across regions which are not attributable to individual or sectoral variation on their own. The remarkable increase in Salvador's wage level since 1970 confirms this proposition, because the productivity gains can be attributed to enormous public investment in infrastructure and an industrial park in that region.

The possibility that price differences could explain the nominal wage differences was not ruled out by cost of living adjustments. It appears that real wage differentials may have converged in the early 1980s. Direct estimation using available price data indicated that real regional wage differences exist, but the hypothesis that real wage differences converged in the early 1980s found support in separate estimates of real wage dispersion. The findings on real wage differentials are not entirely clear due to problems with comparing price levels across regions. The same evidence suggests a divergence in real wages toward the end of the period. Compensating differentials were shown to be an unlikely explanation for nominal or real wage differentials since social infrastructure and amenities tend to be associated with high wage, not low wage, areas.

Finally, another potential source of the regional wage differentials is rents. The annual variations in regional wage differences, however, do not show a strong relationship to short term changes in labour market conditions. If the wage differences reflect rents, then they are not a consequence of temporary fluctuations of supply and demand because these differentials have persisted over long periods of time. Rather, they must derive from a pattern of economic development which continually reproduces relatively 'tight' and 'slack' labour market conditions in different regions.

From the various perspectives on regional wage differentials presented in previous studies, this research shows that regional differentials for comparable workers have not converged over time. These are unlikely to converge so long as the distribution of economic activities and educational opportunities remain spatially concentrated. Instead, the regional wage differentials were more widely dispersed in 1986 and 1987 than at the

137

beginning of the decade. The stability of this pattern must reside in the confluence of two major factors.

First, the agglomeration economies in the São Paulo, along with the low wage level, maintained a concentration of capital and national production in that region, with only moderate trends of deconcentration occurring recently, and largely in response to public intervention. Firms which sell in the national or export markets can reduce their *nominal* cost of labour by moving to the Northeast, but the low wage levels and high cost advantages of established regions make such moves unattractive. This continuing concentration of physical capital, infrastructure and social productivity ensures the persistence of high wage opportunities in particular areas (e.g., São Paulo, Curitiba, and Salvador's petrochemical centre), but only from the demand side. An influx of labour supply beyond the absorption capacity of the economy could erase such wage advantages.

Second, regional differences in labour force composition and growth have been reproduced steadily by Brazil's particular pattern of migration and demographic change. Individuals generally move toward higher wage areas, but even low wage metropolitan regions have continual and significant labour force growth, from both natural increase and migration — from local rural and urban hinterlands. The remarkable expansion of employment in the Northeast in the last decades has been insufficient to absorb increasing shares of the potential labour force (Jatobá 1986). By contrast, São Paulo has largely absorbed the average annual arrival of over 100,000 individuals over the period. Rio de Janeiro represents a special case where migration has contributed to slack labour market conditions over the last two decades — ever since the nation's capital was moved to Brasília — albeit at a decelerating pace. Hence, evidence suggests that regional differences in local conditions of labour supply have reproduced similar conditions over the past thirty years.

It is important to note that these two processes do not mecessarily indicate segmentation of regional opportunities. Rather, they are the result of particular dynamics of social processes allowing the divergence of regional wages to persist over three decades. In a purely market perspective, the wage differences could be eliminated readily by *sufficient* and *rapid* supply and demand adjustments. Individuals do take advantage of higher wage opportunities in other regions, but not at a fast enough pace to offset the continued growth in higher wage opportunities. The particular process, however, which persistently recreates these regional differences in local labour market conditions must be viewed outside of the specific market model. It provides the context within which supply and demand processes operate.

Brazil's spatial pattern of development is the result of highly contingent events. It reflects the confluence of international factors, domestic economic conditions, and public policy. São Paulo's initial rise to dominance has been linked clearly to the success of coffee production during the coffee boom in the world market. But the city's passage toward an industrial centre also depended upon how the income from coffee exports was reinvested (Dean 1969). The persistence of industrial concentration in São Paulo was assisted by decisions to protect domestic industry in the 1950s at a time when open trade might have reduced São Paulo's advantages. The repression of workers in the 1960s and 1970s reduced wage pressures on São Paulo industry, in spite of the enormous concentration of workers in particular areas. It may even have forestalled the potential movement of manufacturers away from this area's concentration of labour organization (Storper 1984). The tentative indications of decentralization in the 1970s can be directly related to public policy, implanting 'development poles' in Salvador (petrochemicals), Carajás (iron ores), and the Centre West (POLOCENTRO); creating fiscal incentives to investment in the northeast and the Amazon (SUDENE and SUDAM); and opening the Free Zone in Manaus.

The dynamics of population movements have also been strongly influenced by contingent historical events. Efforts to promote land reforms in the early 1960s could have stemmed labour force growth in the Northeastern cities of Fortaleza and Recife had they not been decisively reversed by the military coup. Without the drought in the early 1980s, the number of workers available in Fortaleza would have been reduced. On the other hand, without government employment programmes, the impact on wages in Fortaleza could have been much stronger.

Finally, the recreation of differences in local labour market conditions occurs within particular labour market institutions which introduce rigidities and set processes in motion which reinforce the regional wage gaps. When the labour movement emerged from the era of severe repression and began to exercise its renewed (although still limited) power, it was the workers of the organized sectors in the Southeast who benefitted disproportionately. And when 'modern' firms use higher wages to motivate productivity and stabilize their work force, these firms become concentrated disproportionately in the Southeast.

Regional wage disparities persist in spite of the increasing integration of national factor and product markets as a result of the particular spatial dynamics of Brazilian economic growth. This study then substantiates the need for further exploration of (1) the main contextual factors within which wage determination takes place: regional cost advantages, population dynamics, and institutional variation; and (2) the evolution of wages under labour demand and supply conditions within a historically fast-growing, high-inflation economy.

Implications for public policy

The implications of regional wage differentials differ significantly depending on how they are generated. If the labour market were geographically segmented, then it would be possible to improve income distribution by adopting regionally-specific labour and wage policies. This study has shown, however, that regional wage disparities exist in spite of important links between geographic areas. That is, wage differences persist because of regionally-captured externalities in production and patterns of labour demand and supply conditions which are recreated year after year. The implications for regional policy, therefore, are quite different.

It remains true that public policy can take advantage of the regional concentration of poverty to target poverty programmes. Public services which reduce the cost of living and/or improve quality of life can contribute significantly to the alleviation of regional concentrations of poverty. In terms of labour market outcomes, however, geographically distinct labour policies are likely to be an extremely indirect method of improving social welfare. The relative inefficacy of regional labour policies can be inferred from the stability of regional wage patterns over a period of time in which the federal government was gradually unifying the regionally differentiated structure of minimum wages. The one case in which public policy clearly affected regional wage differences came about through the implantation of a petrochemical pole in Salvador — at an enormous cost which will not be possible to reproduce in the foreseeable future.

Instead, the improvement of work conditions, pay, promotion opportunities, and mobility should be pursued through programmes which encourage all firms, *regardless of location*, to adopt technologies and organizational strategies that take advantage of the motivational impact of high wages. Such policies may be direct, such as enforcing minimum wage laws, or indirect, such as strengthening the labour movement.[1] The regional aspects of a national industrial policy must take into account not only the encouragement of regional growth (which is insufficient in itself, Jatobá 1986) and the implantation of high wage sectors, but also the advantages of sectoral and occupational diversity which make up the complex of higher productivity and pay. Finally, local economic organization needs to be studied more thoroughly in order to understand why self-employment is generally more remunerative than being an employee in some regions (Fortaleza and São Paulo) while it is less remunerative in others (Recife and Rio de Janeiro). If the differences are related to the market structure of product or capital markets, there may be opportunities for public policy to improve wage levels by expanding access to income-earning opportunities in places where these are obstructed.

The implications for public policy are generally to deemphasize the spatial aspects of labour policy and stress instead the sectoral, occupational, and educational aspects of restricted opportunities. Divisions of the labour market which are created by the complex interaction of sectors, occupations, and region, need to be the focus of any policy seeking to expand opportunity and income for Brazilian workers.

Notes

1. For example, until the early 1980s a majority of the workers in one large textile firm worked without official work card status and its associated benefits, at wages below the legal minimum, and for workdays which exceeded the legal maximum. The pressure of the textile workers union, taking advantage of slackened labor repression in this decade, was able to force the firm to regularize work conditions and improve wages (author's interviews in Recife, 1989).

Bibliography

Ablas, Luíz Augusto de Quieroz (1985), *Intercâmbio Desigual e Subdesenvolvimento Regional no Brasil*, Pioneira/FIPE, São Paulo.

Ablas, Luíz Augusto de Quieroz, Alberto Eugenio Guido Muller, and Roberto Smith (1985), *Dinâmica Espacial do Desenvolvimento Brasileiro*, Vol. 1, IPE-USP, São Paulo.

Ablas, Luíz Augusto de Quieroz and Vera Lúcia Fava (1985), *Dinâmica Espacial do Desenvolvimento Brasileiro*, Vol. 2, IPE-USP, São Paulo.

Abramo, Luís Wendel and Roque Aparecido da Silva (1988), 'O Movimento Sindical Metalúrgico em São Paulo: 1978-1986', in Ricardo Toledo Neder, et al., *Automação e Movimento Sindical no Brasil*, Editora Hucitec/CEDEC, São Paulo.

Almeida, Ana Luíza Ozorio de (1992), *Colonization in the Amazon*, 1970-1980, University of Texas Press, Austin.

Almeida, Manuel Bosca (1981), 'Estimação do Estoque de Capital no Nordeste e Sudeste do Brasil - 1970', *Revista Econômica do Nordeste*, 12(2), April-June.

Almeida dos Reis, José Guilherme and Ricardo Pães de Barros (1989), 'Income Inequality and the Distribution of Education: Regional Differences in Inequality', Microeconomics Workshop in Labor and Population, Yale University, March 10.

Amemiya, Takeshi (1985), *Advanced Econometrics*, Harvard University Press, Cambridge,Massachusetts.

Baer, Werner (1964), 'Regional Inequality and Economic Growth in Brazil', *Economic Development and Cultural Change*, 12(3):268-285, April.

Barros, Ricardo Pães de (1988), 'On the Empirical Content of the Formal-Informal Labor Market Segmentation Hypothesis', mimeo, IPEA, Rio de Janeiro, April.

Barros, Ricardo Pães de, and Rosane Silva Pinto de Mendonça (1993), 'Geração e Reprodução da Desigualdade de Renda no Brasil', mimeo.

Batra, Raveendra and Gerald W. Scully (1972), 'Technical Progress, Economic Growth, and the North-South Wage Differential', *Journal of Regional Science*, 12:375-386.

Behrman, Jere R. and Nancy Birdsall (1983), 'The Quality of Schooling: Quantity Alone is Misleading', *American Economic Review*, 73(5), December.

Birdsall, Nancy and M. Louise Fox (1985), 'Why Males Earn More: Location and Training for Brazilian Schoolteachers', *Economic Development and Cultural Change*, 33(3):533-536, April.

Bourguignon, F. (1979), 'Decomposable Income Inequality Measures', *Econometrica*, 47:901-920.

Buarque de Holanda Filho, Sergio (1989), 'Migrações Internas e a Distribuição de Renda no Brasil', *XVII Encontro Nacional de Economia*, 2:1071-1090, ANPEC, Fortaleza, December.

——— (1989), 'Migrações Internas e a Distribuição Regional de Renda no Brasil: 1970-1980', *Estudos Econômicos*, 19(3), September-December.

Cacciamali, Maria Cristina (1983), *Setor Informal Urbano e Formas de Participação na Produção*, IPE/USP, São Paulo.

Camargo, José Márcio (1989), 'Informalização e Renda no Mercado de Trabalho', in Sedlacek and Barros (eds.), *Mercado de Trabalho e Distribuição de Renda: Uma Coletânea*, IPEA/INPE, Rio de Janeiro.

Camargo, José Marcio, Ricardo Pães de Barros and Guilherme Sedlacek (1990), 'Mobilidade no Mercado de Trabalho', presentation at IPEA, Rio de Janeiro, August.

Camargo, José Márcio and Franklin Serrano (1983), 'Os Dois Mercados: Homens e Mulheres na Indústria Brasileira', *Revista Brasileira de Economía*, 37(4):435-447.

Castro, Manoel Cabral de (1988), *Participação ou Controle: O Dilema da Atuação Operária nos Locais de Trabalho*, IPE/USP, São Paulo.

Cavalcanti, Clóvis (1981), 'Employment, Production and Income Distribution in the Informal Urban Sector of the Northeast: The Case of Salvador, Bahia', *Luso-Brazilian Review*, 18(1):139-154, Summer.

Chahad, José Paulo Zeetano (1986), 'O FGTS e as Rescisões do Contrato de Trabalho: Uma Abordagem Empírica', in José Paulo Z. Chahad (org.), *O Mercado de Trabalho no Brasil: Aspectos Teóricos e Evidências Empíricas*, IPE/USP, São Paulo.

Chaloult, Yves (1977), 'Regional Differentials and the Role of the State, Economic-Political Relationships Between the Northeast and South of Brazil', Latin American Studies Program Dissertation Series, Cornell University, No. 70, January.

Considera, Claudio M. (1980), 'Estrutura e Evolução dos Lucros e dos Salários na Indústria de Transformação', *Pesquisa e Planejamento Econômico*, 10(1):71-122, April.

Dabos, Marcelo and George Psacharapoulos (1987), 'An Analysis of the Sources of Earnings Variation Among Brazilian Males,' mimeo, September.

Dean, Warren (1969), *The Industrialization of São Paulo, 1880-1945*, University of Texas Press, Austin and London.

Doeringer, P.B. and M.J. Piore (1971), *Internal Labor Markets and Manpower Analysis*, DC Heath, Lexington, Massachusetts.

Duarte, Renato (1984), 'Criação de Emprego e Renda na Economia Informal Urbana do Nordeste: O Caso de Salvador e Fortaleza', in Inaía Maria Moreira de Carvalho and Teresa Maria Frota Haguette (eds.), *Trabalho e Condições de Vida no Nordeste Brasileiro*, Editora Hucitec/CNPq, São Paulo-Brasília.

Dunford, M. (1986), 'Integration and Unequal Development: The Case of Southern Italy, 1951-1973', in Allen J. Scott and Michael Storper (eds.), *Production, Work, Territory: The Geographical Anatomy of Capitalism*, Allen & Unwin, Boston.

Egler, Claudio Antônio Gonçalves (1986), 'Dinâmica Territorial Recente da Indústria no Brasil - 1970/80', text presented at the National Seminar on Technology and Administration of Territory, Rio de Janeiro, August.

Erickson, Kenneth Paul and Kevin J. Middlebrook (1982), 'The State and Organized Labor in Brazil and Mexico', in Sylvia Ann Hewlett and Richard S. Weinert (eds.), *Brazil and Mexico: Patterns in Late Development*, Institute for the Study of Human Issues, Philadelphia.

Fields, Gary S. and T. Paul Schultz (1980), 'Regional Inequality and Other Sources of Income Variation in Colombia', *Economic Development and Cultural Change*, 28(3):447-467, April.

Fishlow, Albert (1972), 'Brazilian Size Distribution of Income', *American Economic Review*, May.

Gomes, Gustavo Maia (1986-88), 'Recessão e Crescimento nas Economias Brasileira e Nordestina,' *Revista Pernambucana de Desenvolvimento*, 12(2):385-399, Recife.

Gomes, Gustavo Maia, Carlos Osório, and José Ferreira Irmão (1985), *Recessão e Desemprego nas Regiões Brasileiras*, PIMES, Recife, February.

Guimarães Neto, Leonardo, and Aldemir de Vale Souza (1984), 'A Dinâmica do Mercado de Trabalho Urbano no Nordeste', in Inaía Maria Moreira de Carvalho and Teresa Maria Frota Haguette (eds.), *Trabalho e Condições de Vida no Nordeste Brasileiro*, Editora Hucitec/CNPq, São Paulo-Brasília.

Hansen, Eric R. (1990), 'Agglomeration Economies and Industrial Decentralization: The Wage-Productivity Trade-offs', *Journal of Urban Economics*, 28:140-159.

Hasenbalg, Carlos (1979), *Discriminação e Desigualdades Raciais no Brasil*, trans. Patricia Borgia. Edições Gerais, Rio de Janeiro.

Heckman, James J. and V. Joseph Hotz (1986), 'An Investigation of the Labor Market Earnings of Panamanian Males: Evaluating the Sources of Inequality', *Journal of Human Resources*, 21(4):507-542, Fall.

Hendry, David F. and Robert C. Marshall (1983), 'On High and Low R^2 Contributions', *Oxford Bulletin of Economics and Statistics*, 45(3):313-316, August .

Hoffman, Rodolfo, coord. with Antônio Luis James and Ana Lúcia Kassout (1990), 'Modernização e Produtividade da Agropecuária em 332 Microregiões Homogêneas do Brasil em 1975 e 1980', Relatório de Pesquisa, CODEVASF/USP-Piracicaba/FEALQ, February.

Humphrey, John (1983), *Capitalist Control and Workers' Struggle in the Brazilian Auto Industry*, Princeton University Press, Princeton.

Jatobá, Jorge (1986), 'The Labor Market in a Recession-Hit Region: The North-East of Brazil'. *International Labor Review*, 125(2):227-241, March-April.

Kon, Anita (1989), 'Considerações Sobre as Diferenças Regionais da Estrutura Ocupacional Brasileira', *XVII Encontro Nacional de Economía*, ANPEC, Fortaleza, December.

Lam, David and Deborah Levison (1989), 'Declining Inequality in Schooling in Brazil and Its Effects on Inequality in Earnings', Research Report No. 89-163, Population Studies Center, University of Michigan, November.

Lam, David and Robert Schoeni (1990), 'Effects of Family Background on Earnings and Returns to Schooling: Evidence From Brazil', text presented at IPEA, Rio de Janeiro, June.

Lang, Kevin and J.S. Leonard (1987) (eds.), *Unemployment and the Structure of Labor Markets*. Basil Blackwell, New York.

Lanzana, Antônio Evaristo Teixeira (1987), *Diferenciação de Salários na Economia Brasileira: Uma Análise do Periodo 1960-1983*, IPE/USP, São Paulo.

Lehmann, Rainer H. and Robert E. Verhina (1986), 'Educação e Obtenção de Empregos Industriais no Brasil: Para um Modelo Causal Aprimorado', *Pesquisa e Planejamento Econômico*, 16(3):631-646, December.

Lerda, Juan Carlos (1986), 'A Política Salarial do Período 1979/85: Alguns Aspectos Dinâmicos', *Pesquisa e Planejamento Econômico*, 16(2):467-492, August.

Lopes de Almeida, Fernando (1982), *Política Salarial, Emprego e Sindicalismo 1964/81*, Editora Vozes, Petrópolis.

Luque, Carlos Antonio and Jose Paulo Zeetano Chahad (1985), 'Formação de Salários no Brasil: Uma Contribuição ao Debate', *Estudos Econômicos*, 15(1):37-46, January-April.

Luque, Carlos Antonio (1986), 'Estrutura Ocupacional e Rotatividade de Mão-de-Obra', in José Paulo Z. Chaha (org.), *O Mercado de Trabalho no Brasil: Aspectos Teóricos e Evidências Empíricas*, IPE/USP, São Paulo.

Macedo, Roberto B.M. (1974), 'A Critical Review of the Relation Between the Post-1964 Wage Policy and the Worsening of Brazil's Size Income Distribution in the Sixties', *Explorations in Economic Research*, 4:117-140.

――― (1986), 'Diferenciais de Salários entre Empresas Estatais e Privadas: Novos Resultados', *Estudos Econômicos*, 16 (Número Especial), São Paulo.

――― (1986), 'Wage Differentials Between State and Private Enterprise in Brazil', mimeo, presented at XII International Congress of the Latin American Studies Association, Boston, October.

Maia, Rosane and Rosângela Saldanha (1989), 'Política de Salário Mínimo: Uma Questão a Ser Equacionada,' in Guilherme L. Sedlacek and Ricardo Pães de Barros, ed. *Mercado de Trabalho e Distribuição de Renda: Uma Coletânea*, IPEA/INPES, Rio de Janeiro, Monografía No. 35.

Martine, George (1989), 'A Explosão Demográfica', *Ciência Hoje*, 9(51):29-33, March.

Mathur, Ashok (1982), 'Regional Development and Income Disparities in India: A Sectoral Analysis', *Economic Development and Cultural Change*, 31(3):475-506, April.

Medeiros, José Adelino de Souze (1982), *Alcance e Limitações da Teoria do Capital Humano: Diferenças de Ganhos no Brasil em 1973*, IPE/USP, São Paulo.

Meneghetti Neto, Alfredo (1988), 'O Efeito da Variável Distância na Migração Interna Brasileira: Algumas Considerações', *XVI Encontro Nacional de Economia*, Vol. IV, RS: Gráfica e Editora NBS, Ltda., Porto Alegre.

Menezes, Wilson F. (1988), 'Parcela Salarial na Indústria de Transformação do Brasil: 1970-1981', *XVI Encontro Nacional de Economia*, Vol. IV, RS: Gráfica e Editora NBS, Ltda., Porto Alegre.

Merrick, Thomas W. and Douglas H. Graham (1979), *Population and Economic Development in Brazil, 1800 to the Present*, Johns Hopkins University Press, Baltimore.

Milone, Paulo Cesar (1988), 'Uma Análise Econômica da Migração no Brasil', *XVI Encontro Nacional de Economia*, Vol. IV, RS: Gráfica e Editora NBS, Ltda., Porto Alegre.

Mincer, J. (1974), *Schooling, Experience, and Earnings*, Columbia University Press/NBER, New York.

Mitchell, Simon (ed.) (1981), *The Logic of Poverty, The Case of the Brazilian Northeast*, Routledge & Kegan Paul, London, Boston, and Henley.

Morley, Samuel (1983), *Labor Markets and Inequitable Growth: The Case of Authoritarian Capitalism in Brazil*, Cambridge University Press, Cambridge.

Morley, Samuel, Milton Barbosa, and Maria Christina C. de Souza (1979), 'Evidence on the Internal Labor Market during a Process of Rapid Growth', *Journal of Development Economics*, 6:261-286.

Murphy, Kevin M., Andrei Shleifer, and Robert Vishny (1989) 'Income Distribution, Market Size, and Industrialization', *Quarterly Journal of Economics*, 104(3), August.

Ócio, Domingo Zurran (1986), 'Salários e Política Salarial', *Revista de Economia Política*, 6(2):5-26.

Pastore, José and Hélio Zylberstajn (1988), *A Administração do Conflito Trabalhista no Brasil*, IPE/USP, São Paulo.

Pfefferman, Guy and Richard Webb (1983), 'Poverty and Income Distribution in Brazil', *Review of Income and Wealth*, 29(2):101-124, July.

Psacharapoulos, George (1987), 'Earnings and Education in Brazil: Evidence from the 1980 Census', Discussion Paper, Education and Training Series, World Bank, Washington, DC, June.

Rocha, Sonia (1988), 'Linhas de Pobreza Para as Regiões Metropolitanas na Primeira Metade da Década de 80,' *XVI Encontro Nacional de Economia*, Vol. IV, RS: Gráfica e Editora NBS, Ltda., Porto Alegre.

——— (1989), 'Incidência de Pobreza nas Regiões Metropolitanas na Primeira Metade da Década 80', IPEA/INPES, Rio de Janeiro, Texto Para Discussão Interna, No. 116, August.

——— (1990), 'Caraterização da Subpopulação Pobre Metropolitana nos Anos 80 - Resultados de Uma Análise Multivariada', *Revista Econômica Brasileira*, 44(1):35-52, January-March.

Saboia, João (1989), 'Salário e Produtividade na Indöstria no Longo Prazo', *XVII Encontro Nacional de Economia*, ANPEC, Fortaleza, December .

Sahling, Leonard G. and Sharon P. Smith (1983), 'Regional Wage Differentials: Has the South Risen Again?', *The Review of Economics and Statistics*, 65(1):131-143, February.

Savedoff, William D. (1992) 'Regional Wage Differences in Brazil's Urban Labor Markets', doctoral dissertation, Boston University, Boston.

———— (1991) 'Wage Dynamics in Urban Brazil: Evidence of Regional Segmentation or National Markets?' *Revista de Econometria*, 11:2, November.

———— (1990) 'Os diferenciais regionais de salários no Brasil: segmentação versus dinamismo da demanda,' *Pesquisa e Planejamento Econômico*, IPEA, 20:3, December.

———— (1987) 'Regional Wage Differences in Guatemala', Boston University, mimeo.

Schmertmann, Carl (1988), 'Self-Selection and Internal Migration in Brazil', PhD Dissertation in Economics, Berkeley.

Schmitz, Hubert (1985), *Technology and Employment Practices in Developing Countries*. Kent, Croom Helm, U.K.

Schwartz, A. (1973), 'Interpreting the Effects of Distribution on Migration', *Journal of Political Economy*, 81:1153-1169, September-October.

Sedlacek, Guilherme, Ricardo Pães de Barros e Simone Varandas (1988), 'Um Análise da Mobilidade no Mercado de Trabalho Brasileiro: Perspectivas de Segmentação,' *XVI Encontro Nacional de Economia*, Vol.IV, RS: Gráfica e Editora NBS, Ltda., Porto Alegre.

Shorrocks, A.F. (1980), 'The Class of Additively Decomposable Inequality Measures', *Econometrica*, 48(3):613-625, April.

Singer, Paul (1982), 'Crescimento Econômico e Distribuição Espacial da População', *Revista de Economia Política*, 2/3(7):31-52, July-September.

Smith, Russell E. (1986), 'Indexação Salarial, Rotatividade, e Variações de Salário Nominal nas Indústrias Textile e de Borracha no Estado de São Paulo — 1966/76', *Estudos Econômicos*, 16(2):227-241, May-August.

Souza, Aldemir do Vale, and Tarcísio Patricio de Araujo (1986), 'O Complexo Petroquimica de Camaçari e o Emprego Urbano', in Jorge Jatobá and José F. Irmão (org.), *Estado, Industrialização e Mercados de Trabalho no Nordeste*, PIMES, Universidade Federal de Pernambuco, Recife, Série Estudos 14.

Souza, Paulo Renato and Paulo Eduardo Baltar (1983), 'The Minimum Wage and Wage Rates in Brazil', *Brazilian Economic Studies*, No. 7, IPEA/INPES, Rio de Janeiro.

Stiglitz, J. E. (1987), 'The Causes and Consequences of the Dependence of Quality on Price', *Journal of Economic Literature*, 25(1):1-48.

Storper, Michael (1984), 'Who Benefits from Industrial Decentralization? Social Power in the Labor Market, Income Distribution, and Spatial Policy in Brazil', *Regional Studies*, 18(2):143-164.

———— (1985), 'Reply', *Journal of Regional Studies*, 19(1), February.

Taylor, Lance et al. (1980), *Models of Growth and Distribution for Brazil*, Oxford University Press, New York.

Thomas, Vinod (1982), 'Differences in Income, Nutrition and Poverty within Brazil,' World Bank Staff Paper, Washington, DC.

———— (1987), 'Differences in Income, Nutrition and Poverty in Brazil,' *World Development*, 15(2), February.

Williamson, Jeffrey G. (1965), 'Regional Inequality and the Process of National Developoment: A Description of Patterns', *Economic Development and Cultural Change*, 13(4) Part II, July.

Willmore, Larry N. (1987), 'Controle Estrangeiro e Concentração na Indústria Brasileira', *Pesquisa e Planejamento Econômico*, 17(1):161-190, April.

Velloso, Ricardo Cicchelli (1990), 'Salário Mínimo e Taxa de Salários: O Caso Brasileiro', IPEA, Rio de Janeiro, Texto Para Discussão Interna, No. 192, August.